COLLECTED POEMS
1975-2015

ACKNOWLEDGEMENTS

Some of these poems have appeared in several journals including *Agenda*; *ArtsEtc* (Barbados); *Bim*; *Callaloo*; *Carib Arts*; *Catholic Chronicle* (St.Lucia); *EnterText* (UK); *Poetry Wales*; *Prairie Schooner*; *Review 81*; *Savacou*; *Small Axe*; *The Crusader* (St. Lucia); *The Ekphrastic Review*; *The Missing Slate*; *The New Voices* (Trinidad & Tobago); *Touché* (St. Lucia); *Trinidad & Tobago Review*; *Wasafiri* (UK); *World Poetry Portfolio #58* (*Molossus*) and in a number of anthologies.

This collection includes work from earlier titles of the author: *Vocation and other poems* (1975), *Dread Season* (1978), *The Prodigal* (1983), *Possessions* (1984), *Saint Lucian* (1988), *Clearing Ground* (1991), *Translations* (1993), *Artefacts* (2000), *Canticles* (2007), *Elemental* (2008), *Sighting* (2013) and *City Remembrances* (2016).

Thanks to:

Cover art: 'The Merchant' by Gary Butte, 2011. Courtesy, Nancy Cole-Auguste.

Author Photo: Davina Lee

Kwame Dawes, Jeremy Poynting, Peepal Tree Press, Msgr Patrick 'Paba' Anthony, The Folk Research Centre (St. Lucia).

JOHN ROBERT LEE

COLLECTED POEMS
1975-2015

PEEPAL TREE

First published in Great Britain in 2017
Peepal Tree Press Ltd
17 King's Avenue
Leeds LS6 1QS
UK

ISBN 13: 9781845233518

Supported using public funding by
ARTS COUNCIL
ENGLAND

CONTENTS

In memoriam: Derek Walcott
1930-2017

For
Veronica
Davina, Esther, Kamara, Richard, Hunter
for
Patricia Ellen Charles 1936-2010
and
Charles Cadet,
and for all the poets of my life.

"...*as we age we both live in a different world, and become different men
in the same world.*" — *T. S. Eliot*

"*So much to do still, all of it praise.*" — *Derek Walcott*

"*Seek ye first the kingdom of God, and His righteousness; and all these
things shall be added unto you.*" — *Jesus Christ (Matthew 6:33).*

MOMENTS
(for Theo)

Nothing depresses so much as when, caught
suddenly unawares, the heart and memory

come face to face and find forgotten pain
in a remembered glance or touch that sought

to ease that very hurt. And when, in vain
later, one tries to fill some emptiness

with some moment that the heart should leave to
memory, nothing depresses so much.

SKEETE'S BAY, BARBADOS
(for Wayne Redman, d. 1978)

One always missed the turning, but found in time
the broken sign that pointed crookedly, loth to
allow another stranger here. Perhaps this Tom
or Dick has plans for progress that will tow
the boats away and make them quaint; that will tame
this wild coast with pale rheumatics who tee

off where sea-egg shells and fishermen
now lie with unconcern. Naked children
      and their sticks flush crabs from out their holes
      and a bare-legged girl, dress in wet folds
wades slow towards a waning sun.

The sea rose angrily.
It knew that freedom here was short.
It remembered other coasts
made 'mod' by small-eyed men in big cars.

And as before, it knew she'd vanish,
the bare-legged girl; the children and their crabs
would leave, a 'better' world would banish
them to imitation coconut trays.

But those small eyes reflecting dollar signs
have not yet found the crooked finger to this peace;
and down the beach the women bathe their sons
who'll never talk, like Pap, of fishing seasons past.

Only memory will turn down this way
when some old man somewhere recalls his day
on this beach where sea-egg shells once lay.

AN ANNIVERSARY: FOR PAUL LAYNE (1945-1971)

"...others are sure to come
as we are an ageless line...(Michael Foster 1945-1965)

I.

I mark now a year, one day
since you became a memory
significant to those you touched.
I mark, too, increased regret
for hours lost, that in an early
morning's sudden call as suddenly
seemed stripped to tragic unimportance.

And for the millionth time (if
still so few) I try to see
your mashed-up corner of my world.
And one more time I now confess
my shameful rude invasion
and callous prostitution
of all instants
that had not shed themselves
of consequence.

II.

And, I confess an indignation
being left
a kingdom of dreams that I must soon make real.

With your other heirs
I must wake our snoring people
from their stale visions.

Yet, fatherfriend, despite my complaints
fearful joy
is what my truly eager soul feels deep down.

III.

I mark now a consciousness of sons to come.
Literacy browsing through some dusty shelf
may find the folder boldly inked COLLECTED WORKS.
Now, too, it seems to breathe more closely than some
one year, one day ago.
        In my verse, a self
            that seems quite out of place, some quirk
of gloomy influence perhaps, more frequently appears.

And now, I mark, one year, a day...

AUTOGRAPH OF A DEAD BLACK POET

(for Victor Questel 1949-1982)

Separating
dying pages with an extra reverent care
I opened on his
autograph.
Respectfully, I
traced the browning, patient hand that had sincerely
hoped this present
would bring happiness.

Standing there, with my hand
in his, I felt his confidence,
sensed his stride across
        the white blank world
that tried to
blot him out.

The aging, fading flourish,
defiant,
final,
was like a march
through fragile shadows
of pale ghosts whose spines were slowly falling
dung, finely pressed
through rats' teeth.

In this dark corner
we leave his greatness.

Subdued, I put the book back carefully
among the others on the dusty shelf.

I WANT TO FILL YOU UP WITH WORDS
(for Denis Foster and Robert Morris)

I.

      lost,
I wandered
          down
                  your promises,
and tried to find
something I'd never seen.

      lost,
forever searching faces
in those crowded rooms,
you
were someone that I never heard.

with sand in my toes
and sun in my hair,
my girl sleeping close
and sea everywhere

I found something
or someone
I hope was you.

II.

when the sun is trapped
by clouds that never grew
from
      wisp
          to whiter wisp,
and tedious grey

is no time seen
as riotous green,

                I want to fill you up with words
                that will rush your womb in heat
                and hope.

when the salt, whispering,
quiet
of sand and sea and sinking sun
are civil servants' dreams in travel folders,

                I want you pregnant as syntax
                that fills forms into shape, from
                nothing.

when my girl and I
try love
on ink-marked sheets
behind the secrecy of postage stamps,

                I want to see you sweating blood,
                feet fixed firm, giving me my
                poem.

I want to fill you up with words.

VOCATION

(for Patrick Anthony, priest and folklorist)

And so, despite the whisperings
behind hands clasped in fervent unbelief,
despite the stale, old lady's scent
of righteousness that crawls from
                                        under French soutanes;
despite all that, and more

this is yours, you, your claim on love.

They could have asked. They could have asked
the blue-smoked hills, the country mandolins;
old trembling-nosed, broad-voiced chantwelles
they could have asked; they could have asked tracks lost
but for some village's dying song;
and belle-aire drums
and violons
and moonlit ragged choirs,
could have told and would have told
of what they'd always known:
that like a hidden mountain stream
caught patient swirling past the ages of the land
nothing dims that vision waiting gently:
of calm clean pools below the waterfall.

And I
who share a common celibacy
that priests and poets must endure,
search the purity of syllable
seeking truths you've found;
incensed with love, I make too
that ritual of Word and Gesture,
wrists uplifted, fingers plucking
outward, scratching at this altar,

daring faith and hope, changing them
into some clarity.

LUSCA
(for Derek Walcott)

Moonlit rings I never knew,
their songs, or dances, chances for first gropings in the dark;
never had I known, like you, grandmothers and their days of pride,
chantwelles for this feast-day or that.

You, your early gods were rum-soaked banjo-players,
wanderers of hills and towns, story-tellers, gossip-mongers,
to whom you gave your heart up captive, new each time, to each new
chord,
to each sweet tongue of flute that whistled you past long canoes,
down lonely tracks, to rivers hiding naked among rocks
and frowning rain forests.

You knew of old crones *dégagé,*
of strange and silent single men who, they said, might have
mounted you,
you dear Lusca, in their *magie noire*! You knew as I did not
of soucouyants and loup-garous, of kélé and kutumba,
of chembois and obeah!

Books could make me fear the dark, but your grandmother,
head scarved, nostrils flaring, could flame her mist-ringed eyes
and send you quick to bed or straight to father-priest's confessional:
    — *Duh lajablesse is coming!*
        — *M'sieu Luwoi et Papa Bois!*
            — *Look! duh screaming faceless Bolom
            searching for Ti Jean and Lusca!*

And so, dear Lusca, I have a loss to claim:
my friends must know that town-bred as I am,
my hands are soft, my feet cling poorly to the land,
my fingers scratch in vain, my toes itch for shoes to wear;
here, I am Lusca's lover, nice boy, but still from town.

The earth will not be entered by my hoe, it cannot conceive
that I can truly want its syllables of roots, its language
of firm green shoots that climb from it with confidence and trust.
A stranger here, my seeds grow weak-kneed, if they grow, and lack truth.
No one believes them, their garbled pidgin making them the village idiots.

       And this is why, dear Lusca, I must remain a lover,
and have but safe acquaintance with your past.
Or every image in your album
will fill me with a morbid lust
when each deserves my gratitude.

       My plot of ground is dry and hard
as sidewalks are; at night street lamps
block out the stars, and hi-fi sets
replace the country violons.
And I must dig foundations deep,
plunge steel and concrete shafts into this city's dirt,
and hope for structures firm,
and spare, no space for flair or show,
each entrance, passage, exit, clear and marked,
each section storing much within a little space.

       Perhaps, Lusca, we should build our house
somewhere on a valley's side, a valley moving
with its riverbed between the country and the town;
then we would see the city's lights
and hear the dying belle-aire drums,
comb the dust of highways off our hair
and smell the burners' blue-smoke pits.

'ITATION
(for Ras Kassa)

My mantra resonant
I fall past my eardrums
and grow
dread

> A black sun's head is
> natted around my eyes
> moving past
> all is thought

Clenched
and teething the wind
face to face with time
words snapped away
broken

> and they recede
> But you
> face to face with time
> the guerilla in the mind
> the cultural revolutionary
> imploding into leather, wood and steel
> making form and shaping all your thought.

DREAD

(i)
On nights like this dark hills take pause; humped knobs conjure
                        to streaming sky,
and harboured, safe, night retreats to shallow doormouths of
                        the supine town.
And I, becalmed, gaze from this bridge down on the shabeen whore
            beneath.

No fable this, for I have seen that face burn black with wanting me,
I have watched those eyes grow soft as smoke with passion's warmth.
I have had those slender fingers clutch my face,
have heard those pouting lips swear unrealities.
I have felt those breasts grow full with promise,
and I have waited,
lonely,
long among hills' mists and snare of blue woodsmoke,
have waited love's sweet tonguing flute among the creaking bamboo
                        roots,
have listened vainly to the distant violons,
eared the throbbing drum of earth.
And I have wept my youth upon the giggling mountain stream,
cracked my age between the dry town's ghetto boards,
and come aboard this manhood.

To promise of the magic words of art,
I set off
toward horizons decked with choice.
They would confound this choke-of-dust-filled August hills,
this arid town of vague deceits,
this comedy of public privacies, french-flavoured morals,
withered, thirsting dreamers.
Lost the freedom that I never had
somewhere between the steaming Boulevard and some Dread-full,
            piss-clogged alleyway.

At a kind of middling of age
(when to be as clear as Réduit sand once was is locked
in the glinting secrets of the sky),
still too young for failure, not old enough to know success,
I found myself a metaphor: the homeless prodigal.

I've heard the evening's belling lure me gently back to lighted streets,
                    soft skirts,
tinkling glassware, the instalment plan.
I've heard the wood-doves murmuring tales of dancing hills
                    and lonely valleys too,
heard them moan for bamboo fluting high above the river-bed
where Lusca sits and sings her mothers' washing songs.

But I have made a pact with one whose name I do not know,
with one who waits for me in every dirty dockman's bar,
in every corner doorway where I stop to strike a light.
She is that familiar swinging hip within the crowd,
the profile at the corner of the eye. She is faceless
and as manyfaced as countless memories left at wedge of many dawns.

Maddened when I've stared too long at old men bowed in
                    dark green quiet,
calm upon taut veins of violons,
she is a ball of fire that among the scented sheets strips firm resolve
to limp acceptance of this sole ambition:
        to name her with the clarity of
              certain women's grace
              a child's quick glancing smile.

And I, dread, have come to parched tongues of bays that whispered
                    treacheries
in crevices of brittle, splitting shells of burning brains.
I too have screamed to 'Mountains, hills, come fall on me!'

And I, dread, have come, clutching berth-right in my sweating palm,

have come back to see her sprawled, to see her splayed like this,
to see above that open, vulgar mouth,
        the gently staring eyes that never change with changing image.

Calm,
from Calvary Bridge I watch that face that set me far adrift,
of all whose promises, only this is sure, sure as the charity of this
                        good night, this:
        an old and broken voyager
        eyes all ablaze and tongue gone mad
        drifting onwards to receding shores

(ii)
Join lines of waving palms, and leave the peeling
ardour of the husked-out days; come take your waiting
caravelle, go round the dulling edge of boring incantation;
nailing pride against crude island bark, go up route
to meet the journey's end. May your flooding heart be
harbour to your will. Come, join lines of waving palms
and leave from age to age the changing phases.

(iii)
Between us there are now
so many dead familiar
so many thrusts of life made reap
and early harvest,
between us now, there are so many
vain regrets to founder on;
still too many needs
plunged in sand
lean clear as undecipherable tombsticks,
and mother, now,
as admonitions from those grave
and watching shadows,
now come, one more time,

23

this pulsing vigour of these
so many brand new lives between us.

(iv)
I'm as ancient as I walk.

I have walked
in my time.
See,
even things set themselves.

Come,
we have to go out
and welcome the enemy.

In faded print,
all are equal.

The death mask is forming.

(v)
Because I have flung myself unto the void
and have exploded into stars of nothing
that would shine for you,

I have known the edge.

Because I was confronted, trapped and shocked
between the multiple recurring image
of my needs in you,

I have known the edge.

Outspaced, past waitfulness,
aged out of shape, and because there are no answers,
I scuttle, frantic,
harbouring unbelief.

JOUVERT

In this dread season, I reach for you and hope you well.

To name you, toutwelles burst from palms of the applauding hills,

and at the circle's mouth, this new love shimmering stands.

In tears and desperate fumbling, weary of the mountains' mermaids
                              and their mists,
I reach for you. Symbols harden.

Falling fast to Easter's joyous heights
the weeks are tumbling over Wednesdays.

May noonday's dusty truth remove all shadows,
and root this love, all stark, all knotted,

to its crown of leaves and blossoms.
We move through this steaming kanaval
my arms around your waist; firmly stepping past its heat,

we reach out for the fragile, flashing triumph of the wreaths,
the ultimate calm of the morning dew.

GIRLCHILD

Poised upon the parish priest's baton,
a waiting girlchild ready stands within the first full flushing of the rows,
stands wide-eyed in the passing hush of Monchy hills,
stands pouting paused before her mighty womanhood.

In tomorrow's crossing paths, truth lies with dreadful calm.

O this is an ironic season, this season of blossoms.
It is Time's full season: the bloom and the blown, the ripe and the rot,
                    O the flash and the fade, O...

The country choir's voices rose,
softly stalked the church's eaves
            and burst above the crooked rim of lurching, panting hills.

PAPA BOIS

(for Tim Daisy, Vincentian poet, d.1973)

"You are young, go ask the world,
and when you find no answers
you will return to find me here
an old man
by this river, on this tree.

Go ask the world why broken hearts
never mend the way men say they do,
go ask the world.
Go ask the world why love and friendship
are only things of youth
and not of older age,
go, ask the world.

Go ask the world why good men always meet
with only scorn and hate,
and why the evil rule the world.
Go ask the world, go! Ask the world!

Go ask the world why I am old
in time's eternal youth."

PRODIGAL

(for Kendel and Jane Hippolyte)
'And when he came to himself...' (Luke 15:17)

(i)

Father: "Do you hear, you all,
the brittle, barking ghosts of dogs down Sans Souci?
Do you hear, you all,
the bawling boloms up and down the village streets?
This night is hot wind which is bringing fear
deep inside the bowels.

Do you hear you all,
the beaching breakers which are falling heavy
on the coffins of the land?
Do you hear, do you hear, you all?"

In the dark,
the sailor has wrecked on his own reef.
The house with light is his father's.

In the morning the hills grow light.
The dark clouds take fire,
the fine rain washes all before.
The fisherman returns laden to the shore
the nets are full of fish.
He brings home the son.

Father: "Do you hear, you all,
my soul sings with light!
Do you see, you all,
light dances before my eyes!
Kill the fat cow!
Light up the place!
Fill the chalice!

O sun, as young as my morning's memory,
I ask nothing
I want nothing
I expect nothing.
I accept everything.
Do you hear, you all,
I give thanks continually.

Do you hear, You All, do You hear?"

Without the Father, all is pain.
I have come to the eye of storms.
I seek nothing.
I accept everything.
The peace of the Father is with I.
I give thanks continually.
Do you all hear?

(ii)

                                    come, kneel.
                                  scratch, scrape
                                        dig here
                                 with your hands.
                          beneath this dry ground
                                   is fresh water.

Labourer
man of the earth
teach me the divining certainty within your palms
that I may even now plunge down soft hands
into this heart of dirt and stone
to cup them firmly full around the darkening roots of soil:

rusting cans, coal ashes used to cover over planted seeds
dry antfull sticks that once held up fine pigeon peas
and young tomato plants

dig again with dirty finger nails
throw up and out and far away those worms
that shift here:

down again   down
down past seasons of old yams and sweet potato
down where the fowls cannot go down
                         dig
                         dig
                         dig down into this furrowed flesh
                         and with the rising sun's firm hoe
                         make grace upon this turned up earth

Is this water
on my hands?

                    wash
                    drink
                    give thanks.

(iii)
And man is yet another flower
that buds and bursts and bursts to bud again,
a wondrous sunblossom
that blooms and blows and blows to bloom again,
a cock of paradise,
that preens to flash and fade and fades to flash again —

and in the fade and bud, that blow and bloom, that burst and flash,
this manbird flowers forth to catch the sun

to hold the fire
to fill its petals with the ever lasting light.
Praise God.

(iv)
And now the days drift like turning leaves
in evening's tender harvest, we too are
gathered in our corners, until night sleeves
the hills and buttons them with lamp and star.

We search the silences behind our words
intensely, like doubting lovers.
Each rage is private with its griefs.

Beyond this bloated eggshell of a sunset
beyond the patience purpling our soft evenings:
yesterday was a quick shadow in hot sun
darting at your downcast eyes, startling.
Today is a boarded tomb that in one night
of wild and frenzied shattering
was looted of our sacred skeletons,
and all was laid out in the starin' streets.

How like a hawk that slides along the air
my heart turns hoarse and beats away in fear
above the circling shadow of its longing:
    to plunge within her bosom pure and trusting
    these betraying hands. The perfect prey.
On the sharp edge of morning, meaning hovers,
incoherent as the screeling birds.

(v)
In the middle of the night this howling.
We will have to wait until the morning
papers come to understand that prowling

messenger's lament.
                    Without warning,
this solitary hound which moves about
our dangerous streets before the dawning

hours, now comes to plead with loud devout
insistence right beneath our shutters.
We yearn to know of what he cries throughout

the dark.
        Dear Lord Jesus, what soul utters
with such keening sorrow, gnashing, gnashing
at the night, what soul is lost beneath my shutters?

My life cannot bear this gashing.
It crumbles from my face's edge, crashing

in the middle of the night.

(vi)
Above Soufriere descending early
morning heals the night in sulphur baths
covers over all in fine rain and light,
and among the mists, below the road's steep edge,
within the valley forest, on a clearing ledge,
see Christ, the charcoal burner,
perfection raking wood and leaves
spirit with bare feet of earth.
His sweet blue smoke climbs steady up to heaven.

(vii)
Although it is so hard these days to talk of friendship,
love, and things like that, still, my friend, if you will please to
trust the One who floods our heart with much we cannot
hold within our foolish selves, I pray that He will shape
eternal beauty, love, and holiness upon you,
as even now, woman of Christ,

        you glow, grow and grace
        me with His Power and His Glory.

SIGHTING: EASTER, 1983
(for George 'Fish' Alphonse)

> Love took upon Himself impurities
> to cleanse our love from our
> impurities.
> The present can bless the past.

i.
Death has come to these:

> Walter Rodney, Guyana, 1942-1980. Patriot.
> Bob Marley, Jamaica, 1945-1981. Prophet.
> Victor Questel, Trinidad, 1949-1982. Poet.

So now I'm writing epitaphs and epigraphs
on another Easter Monday morning.
The open tomb, the burning cross, are now all archetypal,
abstracts of suffering —
for what is roasting flesh but an abstraction of the crucifixion,
> a burnt offering?
> (See Titian's 'Martyrdom of St. Lawrence', 1548-1557)

The vision of Christ risen is understanding.
The sharp edge of Word,
truth carved finely by a master type-cutter.
> — By the way: the Easter meditations of a lonely librarian,
> preacher of sorts.
Titian is teaching me the majesty of Messiah,
Jesus of Nazareth, Son of God, Bar-Jehovah!
> (See also, 'Bust of Christ'. About 1532-1534.
> Florence, Pitti Gallery.)

Now that the mornings of adoration are over
it startles us strangely to hear the falling rain in a long season of
> drought.

Let us learn to love each other
for His Name's sake: God, the Son of Man.

He was pure, the Messenger of the New Covenant,
the Suffering Servant, the Coming Judge.

The raised trumpet roosting at the gates will soon commence a brave
    adagio,
strangely aching pits of heart:
    with unmuted joy
    with sharp terror of high places
    with a surging, breaking sadness for someone dearly loved
    with a clarion to holy war.
For those who gird horizons of the heart with fortresses of steel and
    stone,
who bind their provincialism into a peculiar vice,
men without mercy, women without pity,
comes:
    an unreal flourish from deepest innerspace
    a scream of fearful death, globular as dark, in the middle of day
    the utter desolation of an incredible sound.

The Cross of Love has now been glorified.
But a new Reformation is what we need,
a new Restoration,
for the cleansing of the Church
for the cleansing of the Church
for the cleansing of the Church.
Let us pray together. For the cleansing of the Church. In Jesus' Name.
    Amen.

ii.
We allowed ourselves to be mesmerized by the possibility of
    nothingness.
Is this our sin, the matter of all our evil ghosts and ghouls?

— projections of such a nature! as: some profound abyss out
       beyond imaginary knowledge.
Man, there is a reality of creation.
      — If this Grand Icon is a Hollywood façade, we are grinnering
       illusions,
    distractions of nothing,
with not even a dead supernova to explain our nocturnal
       emissions.

At our delicate interfaces of earth
in our rooted pulsations of eternity
Christ is the tactile substance of my livity.
    I man see the Upper Place of Lights and Falling Fire,
    His I-ness.

iii.
And when the ache of my heart broke
upon lost melody makers,
desolated faiths and those stone,
refusing men, those sneering jokers —
even then, you arrived, (a long shower in drought),
You, to gather all the scattering shards of my prayers.

iv.
    Man's seasons of rut and routine:
the rot of creation around the Rock of faith:
    Golgotha's triumph:
        the globular anaesthetic of death
        the Spirit given up
        into the Father's Graceful Hands,
and then, the eyelids opening behind the folds of stone-grey shroud.

O let there be compassion.
Let us care to love each other.

Let us dare to love each other.
The brittle penny of the world's peace is now the only legal tender,
and we yearn beyond our rationed desires.
Like a firework, O God, we burst at the height of our flaming powers,
shatter into brittle sparks of ash, sad remembrances of light that once
        was shooting star,
and abruptly fall away to nothing in the encompassing dark.

O Lord Christ,
that You would come again and show Yourself to us
and show Yourself
and show.

v.
        Often now, I feel the heavy-clogged, grinding teeth of age
tread deeply into my materials.
As banal as the dust upon my books,
spiders knit with quick futile urgency cobweb groynes to hold the brief
        enticements of these dry-rot days together.
We are, as ever, caught in the honey of our lusts, and
our cultures are collapsing.

Christ calls from the Holy Kingdom down to us:
may the pilgrims find the Way
may the pilgrims find the Way
may all the prodigal pilgrims find the King's High Way.

vi.
And, what has this map to do with my *awefulle journie?*
For I had heard the *cadence* of the youth of my regeneration.
I had known intimately the desperate acts of lonely men in
        darkening rooms.
I confess the dangerous indiscretions of my hungry hands.

I have seen the strange ways of priests in the night.
I have been the making of an icon.

      The way to perfection is reverence for God.

In the newsreels of suffering
the first peaks of our generation's deaths,
the new tomb sticks
on the paupers' graves,
men of the people
Questel, Marley, Rodney;
     and the new dictators
     and the new dictators,
their bombs in our cars,
the atrocities in El Salvador's Name.
  In our unfortunate towns, the Volvo and the video, the new visas
     of the bourgeoisie, the new brood;
the professors of words, the baser initiatives,
the Grenada paranoia, the titters in the theatre's sheltered glare;
in this back yard of the Californian with the new expensive games of
     shuttling missiles and ray guns in the stars,
the parallels of compromise, the markets of confusion;

we test ourselves with possibilities of further death.

But this map, this contoured abstract of memory, this poem sighting out
     remembrances,
is a browsing librarian's *itations*,
Saint Lucian,
with illustrations from Titian and other makers of the icon,
spirit-carved features of the Word of God,
so that we might remember. (Amen)

POSSESSIONS
—Luke 21:19

Even though, even though we come to faith in God
we dare not hope to be set free,
to be redeemed to run away from all those good
intentions, to avoid responsibility.
    Plain speaking, but then the times aren't always good for poetry.
    Not for the ordering line, the turning word.
    Not under regimes of democratic anarchism.

For all the workers of this blue-green island,
this mote of a galaxy, this interruption of an earth,
for all: the deep encroaching dark,
the spectres of regret, the smoking wicks of faith.

So, even though we know that God is love
like the alcoholics of our towns' despair
we all are derelicts of pain
resigned to the crutches of fear
disputing over ulcers, vainly hungering
for pity, our need as relentless as cancer,
even though we know.

The times aren't good for poetry or for faith.
By faith and poetry twice exiled,
seeking responsibility for too many loves,
and because,
because I've called to Christ,

I pray, O God, for the simple faith of a simple man.

And being warned
and being warned of the cities' death by fire,
all that is left us now is careful patience,
that stubborn heart of love, hope, faith,
of the ordering line, of the turning word.

URBAN PASTORAL

(for Lorna Goodison)

i.
out that black hole of bush
have spewed this bouldered hush
of slipping stream, this pushing
back of roots. And women washing.

ii.
a new clear view for today:
far from the Pentagon, this two by four,
and your copra in the blistering heat,
and below the blasted trees, your
childrens' bodies falling out.

or again:
the outboard of your faith, the
nets of the years' woven strengths,
the safe bay of familiar sand, all
gone to nothing. With our sky.

iii.
may the pride of the Old and the New not forget
that out of these rejected Nazareths
still come the Bread and the Fruit and
the Eternal Coal of the childrens' faith.

iv.
and in the mean time,
between August hurricanes,
on the road to Canaries:
    joy is an exalted evening of silver skies come out of childhood time,

country road ever winding back and forward, on among guavas
                    and cedars;
  how to tell absent friends of lambs on hills
  doves in bamboo, our faces
  washed in dew-wet leaves and fern
  our souls set free at last to kneel,
    to kneel O Holy Spirit of our songs
on the road to Canaries?

STAGE: AN EPITAPH

(for Bob Marley)

Corner-stoned
solid now on his times
he's fixed himself
with other figures and their history
on the shifting borders of our soul.

(Was he real, I mean, really?
or did we together pick the pieces in imagination
flesh ambition into form
and stroking all the memories that pad our minds
make ourselves an elegy?

Did some body die?
Or are we preparing now to put away another time
another age that we had peeled
and pinned up
from off our wrinkling hearts
seeking out eternal fixity?)

In truth
a man lived
a man wailed
words flashed in light:
that man pulled poems from his breast
and drew blood.
This man laid his axe to the roots of our faiths
in hope of freshening love.

As we lay him down past our reflections
as we press ourselves into our place
as we settle to our comfort
we draw the shades around our tears
we send the children out
to pick themselves
flowers, herbs, roots.

CHALLENGER
(for G.F.)

In memory of Christa McAuliffe and the astronauts who perished,
January 28th, 1986.

0.07
Christa! Your name implodes,
compressing thoughts in dread significances –
I probe the glittering shards of their meaning
hoping to learn from you,
  down through that deep sea of bewildered grief
  scouring the 'ultimate field experience',
some prophetic conclusion
decisive in impact, whole, not shattered.

0.06
This we share who've shared these forty years:
wars and rumours from Japan down to the Cape,
burning Watts, Martin facing dogs and hoses,
Elvis, Dylan, Marley, all those dead on dope,
the babies torn apart by legislation,
images that Time and Life now bind for us to keep.
All have led to this last frontier,
to that Big Bird cumulus shaping over Florida.

0.05
  America! Howl for all the plunging debris of your sins
raining down upon your daughters and your sons;
on their heads, your pornographies and your abortions,
your dangerous pretence of innocence.
You've mocked the faith that gave you certain strength
and now, the statutes of licentiousness
that frame Los Angeles to weeping Houston
deceive you – proud, and reaching for the suns.

0.04
Now private grief is common currency
how casual we are concerning violence,
taking cable networks' headline news to be
the full accounting of each person's loss –
        till the day Charles Manson's there, before us
        till the day of baby's disappearance,
till that passive winter noon when Christa's
parents stand afraid, bewildered, utterly betrayed.

0.03
So, from the inner city provinces
to southern islands of Amerika,
from uneasy Europe, wary of advances
to Asian peasants hoping on a falling star,
we private citizens admit sorrow.
We do not confess to know the nature
of this strange holocaust. May tomorrow,
Sure Salvation come, removing us from all offences.

0.02
Inevitable as infidelity
tomorrow nears with the apocalyptic
haste of an end of century comet. Tragedy
that is this true makes us talk
less complacently of future shock. We
have all been shown, in modern gothic,
the dark side of boundless possibility,
our creature's vulnerability.

0.01
O, we must go on, our time's conquistadores,
new Elizabethans, adventurers

at the last frontier. Man's quest adorns
both earth and sky in ruins that recur
in every space where he has spent his time.
Cities and metaphors his burning fire
hold, though they fall from use and passing fame.

      Beyond death, last challenger, Christ enthroned.

0.00
(like a fire work, O God,
we burst at the height of our flaming powers,
shatter into brittle sparks of ash,
sad remembrances of light
that once was shooting star,
and abruptly fall away to nothing
in the encompassing dark.)

EULOGY

(for Vic Fadlein 1948-1988)

"*death must not find us thinking that we die*" (Martin Carter)

Outside my window, the insistent bazaar of insects.

There are other sounds: screaming tyres, a dog nagging at the edge
of hearing, a startling shout.

I'm thinking of a recent death,
a friend's, come suddenly.
I can't pretend that we were close,
but some dyings still shake our apathies
though death itself is now familiar.

I keep thinking of this death
which gave that life its meaning.
It marked the place where we've gone over,
this generation he and I have shared.
With him, our youth is truly gone and buried.
Now manhood, and the declension of our times, are left us.

I think he found, in his noontime death,
an importance that he'd always sought.
His death has sounded the alarm
for us lined up behind.
The unbelievable news of his decease
reveals our own unguarded hearts.
Somehow – though there have been other funerals –
this long, dark shroud of mourners
in procession through the streets
seems like a strange birth day
of some emotion
we've not been in before.

Our's a generation come of age,
its fortieth hurricane season,
a generation like all generations,
hopeful, bewildered, proud, careless,
learning hurt, paying its own bills
like all the human race
from which it's learned
the art of coffin-making;
a generation, wrestling with its gods,
with its own heart, with its fathers, and now
with the children
lying in its dying arms.

Yet, this generation
of this island
is unique –
space-age and computer-literate,
advanced in history,
with its own flag and hymn,
    (does that change the ancient bartering ways,
        gossip rolling round the market place,
            buying and selling of power?),
with its own agenda for progress,
even though the World Bank holds the hills in mortgage;
a regenerated nation
who met in forum in the town squares
to talk together for tomorrow's children
and today's ballots;
a new generation who already knew its own betrayals.

My friend, whom I will meet no longer
in the casual boulevards of our city,
whose space is still too clearly vacant
on the market steps, in the union hall,
the newspaper office, on the air,
and in our now more watchful hearts,

my friend, I think, was a servant like all heroes.
He chose to stand beside those other few
who had the courage that is rare
to serve without fear
the needs of those whom blind and foolish men have cursed as poor.

We are another generation,
the inheritors of our parents' secret dreams of revolt.
Yet, the old patois peoples' toil and tears
have now become the substance of our mortgaged properties.
I wonder often if we have not failed them,
those brave, strong, unlettered folk who still remembered slavery.
We have much more
than those godly people ever knew would come to us
in answer to their prayers,
yet we have much less than they
of common courtesies, fidelities, and honesties.

My friend, whose life is now a memory bank I search,
thought deeply, I believe, along these lines.
He chose and walked with labour
following their star, listening to their heart;
he was too old to be foolishly romantic,
he knew the dangers of the frontline
in these paradise facades;
he had responsibilities to home and heart
that were too real for him to play political charades;
        but he was young enough for bravery,
for daring dangerous, corrupting men
too long in charge of killing babies in the womb;
        young enough for anger
that must explode like tear gas in our too complacent streets
before it shrivels up to fear
under public order taxes;
        young enough for love,
a love that is rare, a love for one's people,

48

the true country, the rich fertile earth
of this Saint Lucian human ground.

Outside my window: insects, shrieks, disembodied dogs in heat, dark.

Tyres aspiring over the new highways,
off to the casinos,
or the waterfront highrises, I suppose.

Crimes we'll hear about tomorrow,
deaths we'll hear about tomorrow,
though my friend won't be there
to announce it on the radio.

But in the banana valleys of my country,
in the hills of Marigot,
in the homes of Marisule,
in the understanding of the labouring folk,
in my questing heart,
this death has come to birth a manhood –
a manhood that must set its feet
to march with courage and compassion
on the road my friend has cleared.

At least this common faith I share –
that as my God shall go with me,
I too must serve my people faithfully,
defend their rights to justice, truth and bread,
respect their children and their men,
give honour to their sisters and their wives,
serve them the gifts that they have nurtured,
place before their feet the life they've fed,
speak of Christ, live what He said,

and may my passing be honoured in their sight
as my friend's life is placed among their songs tonight.

AFTER
(for F.N.)

At the end of a track,
our backs to the chastened world,
arrival at the edge,
the flat mercurial sea
and all that's left of earth –

grove of almond trees huddling
like monks in dark habit,
standing still;
beach exhausted
of its burning glare;
lonely regular
haunting something
through the aching clarity
of distant shallows;
left, La Vigie Peninsula,
arrogance poignantly becalmed,
outline familiar all our lives,
sending faithful, cryptic signals
from its lighthouse.

Then, do you see, how,
like swift messengers,
this flock of young birds,
on their first flight from the swamps
in schooled formation, startle,
turn sharp and quick around us,
and return. About their Father's business.

The sky is pure eggshell of afterstorm.
The Sea Gull journeys,
brooding through it, Holy and Sedate.

The slowly scything arcs,
which bear these signs
throughout this marvellous twilight kingdom
that is dawning,
pass out of sight.

Bless us, O LORD.

SANCTUARY

Love is a horizon often lost in haze.

You've learned that you knew nothing.
There were virgins in those days.
Your eyes look on illusions
perpetrated to deceive.

You must wait for the fruit
for the revealing of the trees.

Love, like fragile dew,
doesn't come from nowhere.
        Look, from the ground of our incomprehensible hearts
cleared consistently of parasites,
wet with tears of pardon pleaded for,
ploughed and planted patiently, garnered with respect,
        you may see in the early hours of your prayers
an embracing mist, like those that filled your first house
in the hills, rising,

        and as dawnlight blesses gently mountain shoulders,
slowly slipping off their patterned quilts,

                you will discover love laid down,
                glistening balm for our anointing.

This must be taught to the children.
And since we are such poor examples,
let our sense of helplessness
lead us LORD, towards Your Temple

where the holy, plunging fountains
of Your sacred, broken Heart
wait to wash and wake and heal us,
part by sorry, faithless, part.

GROUND

— Psalm 127

(for Veronica)

Now he is committing to the land.
He deposits in a bank all his labouring years
in exchange for what they'll lend
to own this simple plot of bush, rock-stone, colony of worms.

Now he stands, roots-ready. No more tears
for a far country. He's come to terms.
He will clear ground into space for towers
and guard the loves that age has borne.

Let certainties of doubt make faith a firm
foundation. Fear will be sworn down
in the clearing. Peg squirming
boundaries of hate with iron hand!

Holy be this ground which he has torn
from the encroaching weed. Honed
cedars bind green edges of his gates. Above Monier,
cloud pillars gather. Look out for showers.

Trodding drenched earth, foot in him land,
far bamboo-bird bugling, the man see clear
the raising of him tabernacle, Him standing
in the Sanctuary, peace passing on Him works.

SEED
(for Jesus, the Word)

Plant, seed, in this earth
and die.
Root,
shoot,
spread your lives around you.

Settle, seed, in this ground,
and die.
Burst,
thrust,
claim your shape upon the sky.

       Tree, you are my age in this earth.
       Tree, I am weary of this earth.
       Tree, endure to the end
and I will make of you
an eternal Seed.

EXODUS

Out of the stonebursts, water. Cool, clear, good.

Out of the shattering cloud, fire. Pillar firm.

Out of the tumbling sky, angel food.

Out of our hearts crawled the murmuring worm.

(Mercy, LORD.)

CHURCH

(for Ralph & Judy Kee)

The church is the hand of God in the world.
The church is the claim of God on His own.
The church is the eye of God on pride curled

within the secret place. Let us search in
our new life to find the church of Christ:
does His healing care pour abundant on

my neighbour? Does His banner crown the crest
of all my mournings? Has the hiding rebel
knelt with tears before the throne of grace?

Ancient rites of water, holy table
bread and wine, shedding blood, sacred prayer, still weld
the living stones who make visible

His great mercy, love, patience, with earth's wild.
The church is the hand of God in the world.

REPORT

When I returned from dinner
just after twelve,
the screaming absence of my radio
from its bedroom shelf
stopped me. Baffled, my mind groped to comprehend.
"I've been robbed!"
The incredible thought
rang my ears,
raised my hairs,
battered down my heart.

In the library,
the window emptied of its louvres
leered black,
mocking Lee.
The thief
had stolen into the house
by climbing up a backyard drain-pipe.
A frantic search exposed other empty spaces.
Fear howling through my throat,
prayer putting up barricades,
I raised the neighbours.
We went for the police.

That damned thief
has spoiled the air in which I live.
I had been violated, my defences
penetrated.
I think: he walked in here,
into my room, my inner chamber,
where I let go my self,
where my loneliness unmasks,
my confessional;
he must have spied on me,

plotted to force himself on me,
deliberately, to steal, to grasp,
to take what is not his.

He must have moved swiftly,
damned thief,
haloed in darkness,
ears nervous for discovery,
desecrating all my private corners.

                    (Faith becomes shifty-eyed.)

My Toshiba radio, companion in divorce,
my Chinese clock, gift from my mother,
my Seiko watch, needing repair,
a travelling bag,
my bus-fare coins,
and I still have to find
what else is gone.

It took three weeks,
but now the house is more secure,
and though sounds at night
can make me apprehensive,
I've placed the thefts
among those other possibilities
that wait to take us by surprise.

In such strange and painful ways
are we prepared for each day's
remembrances of death,
that damned thief,
always entering unguarded entrances
to bedrooms of our life;
prepared too, for my LORD,
whose coming's been announced,

whose arrival time's uncertain,
but bolted doors and burglar bars
won't keep me from my Saviour's gathering arms.

ARTEFACTS

(for my children)

1. house

When the earth shook
my mother made us
kneel, while she took
her rosary beads

and began to
pray, "Our Father…"
Her Bible was the
first I remember:

its frail tattered
pages glowing under
the hot chimney
of the kerosene

lamp perched on old
books at one corner
of a dresser piled
with miniature

shrines of saints, pow-
der bowls filled with pins
and buttons; bow-
ing, arms extending

in perpetual
kindness, Mary's broken
statue stood as usual
up against

the mirror holding
in its varnished frame
dark partitioning,
the old bed crammed

with mattresses,
bloodstained mosquito
net, the mysterious
black cupboard that

we often
tried to break open. No
pictures. Out of view
my father's low

single bed on which
I must have knelt to
read, at the edge
of my mother's

dresser. In those
days, the house was three
rooms. A front place
with a table that we

hardly used. It
was my father's. A
gothic cupboard that
held plates and un-

used glasses. A couple
chairs. Doors and windows
carried double
jalousies whose

dustfilled flaps were
agony to clean.
We slept together
in between

the front entrance
and the back room where
tables and trunks
were stored for years.

Conrad Lee, grand-
father I never
knew, Barbadian,
worked in Panama,

had built this house.
After the forty-
eight fire, when his
wife had lost every

thing she had, my
father brought them here
to La Carrière:
welcome, poverty.

I was six weeks
old when the fire flattened
Castries. So quick,
overnight, a rotten

era fell in
upon itself. My
mother lived on
Coral Street. Her me-

mories of all
she'd lost: her status,
her things, her full
inheritance,

embittered her.
Her father was well-
known among the
town druggists; it fell

to her to take
the business over
(during the war),
when he died. Vic-

tor, her famous
brother, was a teacher
in Grenada.
From her garrulous

halfsister, my
Auntie Eileen, I
heard the rumour
of quarrels a-

bout property.
Romance with Alleyne
the greyeyed sea-
man, Anglican man,

split the Archers
from my defiant
mother; for years
her brother wouldn't

meet or talk with
her. Alfy Joy married
Lee – with what
must have seemed mad re-

bellion, she went
against the vain browns,
against the sense-
less hates around

her, against prized
class stupidities
of the doomed priest-
ridden town. That they

foundered later,
her greyeyed sailor,
their scorched schooner,
on hard La Carrière,

made her even
more a child of our
fractured, lost cen-
tury. Open air

Joy, in love with
the sea, losing faith
in the ash waste
of Castries, preferred

the closed jalousies
of that dark room they
came to, sleep-filled days
that kept self pity

alive like bugs
in the coconut
fibre. They bogged
down, stubborn. Each put

the blame for loss
of what they had before
on interfer-
ing families.

Those were the days
when I first knew them.
They had three boys.
A lost dying flame,

temporary
truce, went out in fif-
ty five when baby
Joel died. Aft-

er that, there was
nothing. Alleyne learned
patient silence.
Joy, bitter, interned

herself in dark
pride and nagging de-
feat. We'd embark,
sometimes, on rare journeys

to the beach with
Joy or Alleyne. In
that tongueless growth
under mangoes and

oranges, off
Vide Bouteille Rd., near
Raymond's bread shop,
I learned to bear

silence, to hear
the spirits of leaves
brooding as they
turned their quiet lives

around, under
my mother's smoking
lamp. Tender vir-
gin quiet stroked

my baffled hurting,
as we four found
our lives, unshifting
crotons rooted in

strange peace, growing
up.

2. mango

On Sunday afternoons in mango season,
Alleyne would fill his enamel basin
with golden-yellow fruit, wash them in clean water,
then sit out in the yard, under the grapefruit tree,
near the single rose bush, back to the crotons,
place the basin between his feet,
and slowly eat his mangoes, one by one, down to the clean white seed.
His felt hat was always on his head. The yellow basin, chipped near
                                the bottom,
its thin green rim, the clear water, the golden fruit,
him eating slowly, carefully, picking the mango fibre from his teeth,
under those gone, quiet afternoons, I remember.

        Me sitting in the doorway of my room, one foot on the steps
                    that dropped
into the yard, reading him, over a book. That's the way it was.

3. *gramophone*
(for Kamara)

One rare afternoon, full of hibiscus and sunshine,
the jalousies of the covered verandah open
to the quiet life of 12 Trinity Church Road, Grace Evelyn,

grandmother, 'the other mammy', left her kitchen
bench from which she ruled with fierce Choiseul-shabine frown,
from biting the ears of us unruly children,

and on that happy two o'clock, she gathered us around,
Doodoo, Babalee and I, opened up the Victrola
that my father had brought her from down

South, Trinidad, dusted its black and silver
parts, showed us how to clean the heavy 78s with a rag
dipped in kerosene, and as we pinched each other

with excitement, she wound up the gramophone with a grin,
took a shiny record from those on her lap, carefully grooved on the heavy
                                        silver head,
and then, in that gracious hour that has grown

with my life, His Master's Voice dipped and wobbled,
and then, the nasal singer: 'How much is the doggy
in the window, arf! arf!' Before that afternoon had

disintegrated, never to form again, before we bogged
down again, in interminable unkindnesses,
unforgivenesses, stupidities, silences, we begged,

and she spun us more of those crooners:
'O my papa', 'My bonnie lies over the ocean', 'Amapola',
'Sweet hour of prayer', 'My darling Clementine'; there was

68

Lord Kitchener, and perhaps, 'Jean and Dinah,
Rosita and Clementina' by young Sparrow. Now
memory blurs as I reach for more

of those wiped 78s on her lap I know
I heard, that have left an echoing nameless tremor
on my soul's childhood, still, somehow,

humming in me. I seem to have had a number
of those single epiphanies, once taken shape,
once dissolved, gone forever:

my mother picking out the grey
hairs from my father's head; friends
coming to our house under the mango trees to celebrate

my second (shortlived) brother's christening; my father, intense,
whispering at me out of his vision, 'the first-born belongs to the Lord';
that time he and Mr. George, his friend the mechanic, spent

all day rigging up a huge, noisy dynamo, electric cord
all over the place, to play his handsome Grundig radio.
When at last it crackled static and we heard

the voice, it made the news I paraded
to Gabriel Mondesir and my mates at school
for days. Once, on Trinity Church Rd.,

when a clatter of running feet drew
us to the windows and jalousies, my cousin Babsy
laughed out: 'McDonald Dixon, that mad fowl!' But, in truth,

that afternoon with Grace Evelyn, everyone busy,
the house left to us and her,
dips like a golden hologram, not easy

to hold in all its wobbling dimensions. At the centre
that sad, collared pup, making me dizzy,
whirling round and round and round, bent head alert,

searching forever down the silver horn of his Victrola, kerosene-
polished, and we gaze at the undulating songs, not caring what they
mean.

4. city

Well, ba-bye to all that. I must arise, Luke, from sipping
        coffee at Warburton's, browsing at Brattle's Life-coloured walls,
and go back, to Castries, Saint Lucia, my home. Home. Home. All
        those figures of birth, lineage, growing ambitions, lie
        vaguely on our curriculum vitae and say
        nothing much about what makes us call a city
home. Why we return there. From Boston's distance, I
        gaze at a pretty postcard and recall

my life there: artefacts air-brushed from memory, teasing
        holograms in glass globules, daring translation:
        my father's cluttered drug-shop on Jeremie Street, offering Tisane
        de Bourbon, Sacrool and, if you want, madame, epsom salts, tiel-
                and-camomille with senna leaves, out of deep brown
drawers that ran against the wall, under shelves that boasted jars of
                                Thermogene,
        boxes of Buckley's cough mixture, flat round tins of Vicks vapour
                                rub.
        From behind the safe crest of the high counter,
        we watched the Mardi Gras parades, as they bobbed
up the street, from drifting early stragglers into cruising decorated
                floats. At the hub
        of steel pans, bodies locked to bodies, and lone jouvert
        eccentrics, sat the heart-breaking beauty, Queen of Kanaval.
        Next-door, my neat hair-netted Auntie Ella Evelyn was always
good for bottles of orange Pino and some Paradise Plums from her jars.
                Sundays: comics from the *Trinidad Guardian* —
                        Dick Tracy, Mandrake, Lil Abner;

Walcott's 'Focus on the arts'; late lunch at no.12 Trinity Church Rd.,
        and then Alleyne's slow silent walk up the Darling
        to our home at La Carrière. Accept this grid,
        start with that street that marks my first border of the flooding
heart of Castries, find the shops, Skeete's newspaper store, the flowering

flamboyant at Cherry Corner that will turn you on
to gently rising Church Road. Before I went discovering
the Graveyard off Chaussée, the Morne above Brazil's length,
the Prince Alfred Basin
behind Bridge Street, I knew my father Alleyne's walk up Jeremie,
past Martha Arlain's
grocery, Patrick Vincent's rumshop, the CDC verandahs, the
Market Steps.
What can I make for you of these old bones, these scratched
pebbles?
They will change their shape as memory doubles
back to find them in that fading light.
Why do we return there? No reason

is good enough.

NOTE
(for V.)

i.
Straining on pleasure at every splint of memory,
unsettled with desire for more time with you,
I'm sure I stumble with handicapped patience
through Summer's closing calendar; and do
my sterile fantasies bring you
to the empty frame of my apartment door?
to the cold corner left over in my borrowed bed?
to the rooms furnished without voices?

There is a boundary of hope around tomorrow
like the grey slate of our familiar sea
without a sail around its turning edge.
What conjunctions may occur
when Fall recycles her worn passion
wedge the coordinates of my faith.

ii.
After the last flurry,
the snow gathered like white carnations
on the brown sticks of the bald hedge.

Winter makes reluctant penitents of us all:
the ascetic trees,
in seasonal, gaunt affliction,
bear the losses of Fall;
the men, scrunched into their pockets,
breathe visors of mist,
hide faces in thick shrouds.

We recycle the stark, horrid beauty of debt-filled seasons,
repeating, repeating, repeating boring sins; always,
the naïve grace of young Spring, the scorched youth of Summer's rut,
the fragile sticks of declining Fall, the slush-bound memorials of Winter:
armed treaties, hopes raised on falling walls,
new invasions, new patriots,
new stone slabs before which we'll also stand, dutiful and distracted.

Looking for the Prince of Peace,
Yeshua Hamashiah, the Faithful and True,
we break each day apart,
crumbling with faith
vacant hours between appointments,
at bus stops, in coffee breaks and marriages.
He is not here. He is risen.

He is not here. He is risen
from the vaulting caverns of Manhattan
the commercial crypts of London
the snaking ziggurats of Brussels
the market sphinxes of Tokyo
the burning bunkers of Kuwait
the looted pyramids of Zimbabwe
the frozen catacombs of the Baltics
the poppy fields of Tiananmen Square
the carnival favelas of Rio
the bauxite pits of Kingston
the sulphur craters of Soufriere
the polluted gulfs of Alaska
the choked arteries of Boston.
He is not here. He is risen.

Over Cambridge, Massachusetts, jets part our heaven
into white loaves that tumble casually,
cotton candid, light as cloud,
feeding the Shawmut air.

And the eye begs for signals
the heart kneads visions:
gatherings on distant hills,
ceremonies of eagle feathers,
buffalo horns at the edge of dawn,
beauties of a race restored,
riding of the King on His great colt.

Clearing ground, the Green trolley rings us down Commonwealth
                                      Avenue.
He is not here. He is risen.
He was the fleece-hooded Stranger on our bench,
feeding squirrels in Arlington Gardens,
on His way to Government Centre,
through Haymarket.

TRANSLATIONS
(for Lau & Beth Gomes)

Goodbye, St. Botolph Street —
    already, I love the shaping memory
    of your quiet tributary my unAmerican island feet
    stroll beside when I come into you off Mass. Ave's frenetic artery.
Your trees have white small flowers and busy birds again, suddenly,
    with the teasing of temperamental Spring.
    You look like a street I want to live on. I could hold you fondly
    in my first memories of Boston as I do those kindling
remembrances of no.12 Trinity Church Rd., Castries, another place
                    aspiring
    in my heart, under sun, behind hedges, to some hint of order,
    some unattainable, unearthly peace. There is something, though,
    down your unobtrusive sidewalks, across your clean banks of
                  brownstones,
that is a familiar intimation, a promise of something kinder,
    which I must have heard at first, back then, among the red
              hibiscus, whispering.

St. Botolph Street, neighbour, I am leaving —
    How has it been? This Fulbright year? This first Winter?
    Pleasant — somewhat like the deceptive quiet that says nothing of
             the troubled living
    behind your fashionable variety of closed customised bowfronts
             I'll not enter;
guarded — Christ's grace around us like the black wrought-iron fences
    which hedge the tulips and forsythias blushing up the modest
             gardens
    of your inaccessible condominiums; baffling — like dinner banter
    skirting gossip, and you a stranger, given awkward burdens
of casual confidences, meaning nothing. Discovering how many dead-
             end
    roads slip easy off your gracious avenue, St. Botolph,
    sniggers somet'ing 'bout dis cold year for which I haven't found

a name.
St. Botolph, are the streets of America, from Ellis Island to Cam-
bridge just like you: embracing patrician lanes bisecting murderous
thoroughfares
evacuating off themselves to forbidding cul-de-sacs, which move
us on, to bewildering Huntingtons???

Wellington Street is green again —
after the rains, our hedges at no.21 bristle with unruly leaves
though the trees have not yet flowered, like those on St. Botolph's.
When sun comes out, children we have not seen before, their lives
hidden like squirrels in the boles of Winter, litter the sidewalks with
laughs,
clattering skateboards, bicycle feats; when sun comes out,
the old man, bundled fat all season, snoozing among his bundles
near Mass. Ave's
Orange Line underpass, removes his face from heavy cowls
that are as black as his bags, clothes, skin, and there, around
the corner of our street, among pregnant crocuses and tulips, he
unpacks his razor, shaves, and as I go by,
he's laughing with the warmth. I've
seen him on other streets, on those days, cap jaunty,
no bundles, at the corner of a **WALK-DON'T-WALK**, talking loud

among the flashy skirts of traffic. The madness of uncoiled Spring
is beneficient, conjuring fresh green leaves,
multiplying syllables of multicoloured children, stripping
homeless old men of their rags, sending lovers
out to find: blooming sunken forests in the dunes of
Ipswich, dolly-shops of Rockport-by-the-sea,
jugglers in Quincy Market, chess players in the filled cafés
of Cambridge; when sun comes out: students of Berklee
tan the lawns of Mother Church; breaking its leash,
a pup plunges into the Reflecting Pool where someone's left
a toy boat to bob in the eddying turbulence. Under St. Botolph's
flurrying dogwood,
a house alarm is trilling; with

starts and stops, the brown UPS van idles from door to door. A Spring
in the life
of. The young men next door are smoking grass in the tiny park and so

stupid, someone has broken a bottle on the children's sidewalk
back on Wellington Street. Well, soon come,
we're outa here. Goodbye St Botolph. Au revoir Hancock,
pale-blue glass-bolted ziggurat. Mother Church extravagant.
Boston
Common, your forlorn Pitynski Partisans and St. Gauden's frieze of
doomed glory. Tremont
Temple, Downtown Crossing, Filene's Basement, Au Bon Pain.
Fare thee well, South End, Back Bay. So long Davis Square. Hey,
pan-flutes
of Harvard Square, buskers of the underground, see you again
sometime, somewhere, if not in Copley, then my own Columbus Square.
Bunker Hill, proud stone like a finger indexing history, your flat
graves falling
down the hillside over Route 99, I've watched you through the
glass
of the College Library. For ten months we've shared some common
ground, but Charles-
town, old ironsides, will soon be off my list of places to be watchful in.
Until we meet again, 21 Wellington Street, Apt. no. 1, your bare

two rooms filled with borrowed furniture; your marble,
mantelled fireplace, sealed; your hot-air vents that choked
us up, your basement furnace grumbling
into heat as if it wanted to explode; your drafts unchecked
by the landlord's hair-driered-plastic over all the closed
windows. Until. No complaints. We've been safe here, peering out
morning, noon, cold night, at the shut doors and bowfronts, cheek
by jowl, cheek by jowl, monotony of brownstones, and it's
strange, this neighbourhood of strangers, not
ever seeing who it is that lives across the street.
Our LORD's grace has kept us, prayers answered in friends,

food on the table, trouble somewhere else, up the road in Roxbury.
We've seen Winter suck bud, leaf and green
twig into brown knuckled stick. Seen the snow storm eat
cars whole, turn red-brick walks into ice-burgers, knit

neat fleece hoods on to bare morning hedges.
Hustling down the turnpikes, we are forced to stop, to pay our
debts.
More friends went underground this Winter, and we, we tunnel
down the clattering ducts
of subway arteries, comparing death masks furtively in our
crammed
reflections. When we debouch into the warm Spring day, singers

from El Salvador, with violins, pipes and native drums
are dancing in the carnival of pigeons, coffee shops,
police horses, Chinese newspapers, and that dreamy
jingle for Estée Lauder that drapes
itself around all that life, a sweet-toothed, dripping
Johnny Mathis sound, the seducing voice of this downtown world.
Well, ba-bye to all that. I must arise, Luke, from sipping
coffee at Warburton's, browsing at Brattle's Life-coloured walls,
and go back, to Castries, Saint Lucia, my home. Home. Home. All
those figures of birth, lineage, growing ambitions, lie
vaguely on our curriculum vitae and say
nothing much about what makes us call a city
home. Why we return there. From Boston's distance, I
gaze at a pretty postcard and recall

my life there: artefacts air-brushed from memory, teasing
holograms in glass globules, daring translation:
What can I make for you of those old bones, those scratched
pebbles?
They will change their shape as memory doubles
back to find them in that fading light.
Why do we return there? No reason

is good enough.
    Well, *ciao*, 39 Fordham Road, samba gospel,
    high-life charismatics, kwéyòl tambourines, New Life
    Fellowship, the New Jerusalem of Allston. Well
Wadislau, even as the glinting shards of fallen steeples
    wink behind our backs in transcendental New England,
    Christ our LORD is calling from the favelas
    of Babylon the new pilgrims. Boat-lifted, their boulevards
drowned under dictators, debts, disease, they're shored up down in
        Somerville, Dorchester and Mattapan.
    They have home no continuing city, and anchor faith
    in that Citadel alone of sure foundation, beyond Rio, Kinshasa,
        Gonaives, Boston, Castries,
    beyond the excavating turnings of the heart, whose
        promised ease
is glimpsed in this store-front temple you and Ralph have rented,
        renovated,
    printed with your faith, for the redeemed from foreign lands.

Boston, April 1991

80

HOLOGRAM

(for Luke & Barbara Salisbury)

After the roll & tumble, we may find a startling
    company of grandfathers: long obscure poems loaded with secret
    perfections, put away for the quiet retreat of returned prodigals;
    muttering lyrics, once rejected, hold freedoms that we've twisted
    our lives all out of shape to find.

Poems are like children. Conceived in mystery,
    our minds lost in strange passions, they arrive
    to be fussed over, pinched, hugged and worried;
    dressed up, dressed down, straightened out, set clear
    on ways of speaking (they'll bear their own

subtleties & indiscretions, make their own intrigues, stir gossip);
    we compare them to others' children, are aggressive
    for their success, fear namelessness in their failure,
    excuse all weaknesses, despair over their future,
    humiliate ourselves to get them good recommendations.

Then, we fight to let them go, fall where they may,
    make their way, shape their world, talk their
    jargon, hope they'll be found honest. It is certain
    that life's not an open book: the plainest face withholds
    founts of sly metaphor & all sorts of reversing symbol.

Fathers, sheltering stones that revolve in our ancient bones,
    may they make true friends, as I have.
    I commit you to the future with prayers,
    my children, my poems, my friends.

SONGS

(for Frank Norville 1944-2015)

> '*My mother is a rose,*
> *my father is a marguerite,*
> *I myself, I am the root of flowers*'.
> — Sesenne Descartes

i.
Lakonmèt, with banjo, bones, guitar, chak-chak, etc.

Chantwelle:
If I tell you that affair grieved me
you can believe it's true,
if I tell you you tore up my heart,
you can say yes, it's true.
If I tell you you pierced me
you can believe I tell the truth.
Young people of today,
you do not make your love for nothing.

I met you on the highway
I met you there, you were all broken up,
I took you, I brought you to my own home
gave you food, gave you drink.
I took you to the store
bought you all you needed.
Yet you still thought I wasn't doing enough,
you took your bundle and left.

> *Chorus*:
> When I tell you you brought me grief
> you can believe it's true.
> Did I say you tore apart my heart?
> But yes, it's true.
> If I tell you you penetrated me

you got through me
you can say yes, yes it's true.
O the children of today
they find love as nothing.

ii.
Lakonmèt, with guitar, drum, chak-chak, flute, rattling bones.

Auntie Ko, speak to Edward for me.
Auntie Ko, warn Edward for me.
The next time, I'll throw hot water on him.

> "Edward's maman is tired of speaking to him
> Edward's papa has already talked to him
> Edward's family have already warned Edward
> The next time, you can throw hot water on him!"

My mother died and left me a mattress.
That mattress is my treasure, all the riches I have.
Edward passed by and asked me for a sleep on it.
When he was leaving, Edward wanted me to give him a piece!

> Auntie Ko, please, speak to Edward for me,
> warn him, Auntie Ko.
> Auntie Ko, you will speak to Edward for me?
> The next time,
> I'll throw hot water all over him.

(Sesenne Descartes, St. Lucia.
Trans. by J. R. & Veronica Lee)

FROM SILVER POINT, EASTER

(for Llewellyn & Christina Xavier)
Acts 2:32

i

And His extending grace
invites us now to make
Atlantic surf, that slipping
shift of hill shade, those waking

lamps that lace the darkening
hedge of mornes – invites us,
if such benediction draw us – to raise
them from our grateful hearts,

poems, psalms, some framing sketch,
that art His encompassing grace.

ii

While Carème burns Point du Cap
dirt-brown, dusts over
Gros Islet, dries Cas-en-Bas
and Bella Rosa,

pregnant mango trees are
parading blossoms all
along the avenues
winding Morne Monier,

and down yards of little balconies
cascade the purpling cedar.

iii

O Lord Christ, that we might,
with hearts' mouths hushed, see You
take the backyard-oven bread
You share with us, see Your hands

raise that plump loaf up into
this day's lavender end,
know with burning, blessed
sight, it's our Master bends

and breaks those dry-crust ends
of breasts of Paix-Bouche bread.

iv

Near the Boguis River
in the sepulchral dawn
en haut bitassion
a weeping woman,

the labourer climbing
through green banana fronds,
and across their framing hills
hibiscus rose is running,

with bougainvillea
pouring over fences.

v

"From Désbarras through Garrand,
look back on small Chassin
that decorates the skirt
of La Sorcière, choose

that clearing, there, enclosed
by the encroaching trees,
plumed by blue coal-smoke –
know that I John did see

H.I.M. enter the enfolding
silence of that mountain,

vi
the fiery tongue of parting
cloud, the wheeling chariot
of great Ciseau La Mer,
and ascend upon the chanting

of His mighty host, singing
the new psalm of the Lamb,
Almighty Jah – to stand
before the throne of emerald

on the sea of crystal,
to receive the Book,

vii
and loose the seven seals.
I John, in the Spirit
on heights of Fond Assau,
have seen too much to utter,

but till the Holy City
come, O let I husband, Lord,
this earth, these valleys,
Silver Point to Morne Sion,

Anse Galet to Bay Fond D'Or,
this small spot near La Croix Chaubourg."

viii

In the fiftieth year,
watching from Silver Point,
I saw the *lampions* falling
down the Morne upon

Castries, Corinth, Marisule,
and they made a Bird
that opened out Its wings
from Monier to Vigie,

that beaked the evening shallows
under Mount Pimard.

ix

Castries knows the sound
of rushing, mighty wind
under flimsy galvanise
it prays will stay nailed down

when August falls on us —
and the place was urbanised
by the '48 fire
when old corners were lost

from Chaussée to Alfred's Basin,
Brazil to Victoria,

x

but now the streets are filled
with small shops, umbrellas
of sidewalk vendors, coal-
pots of *lambi* and fowl-

wings, cruising Toyotas
that boom dancehall from Kingston,
and the Kwéyòl people
curse Syrian, Tourist,

Guyanese, Martiniquan official,
as Mammon gives them utterance.

xi
Into Choc's shallow pools
wade the elders, while their
assembled flock sing redemption
hymns under the near-

by almond trees and where
those who will be added
to the kingdom stand like shorn,
shy sheep, sheltering and

close, a little awkward
in the tourists' kindly stare.

xii
The saints come to silence,
the elder proclaims
for all the beach to hear
the ancient promises,

and defiant Amens
now lead the candidates
toward the engulfing
tomb whose further gates

open on to hoped-for heights
beyond spluttering belief.

xiii
At the sacramental
table, we remember
Gethsemane's sorrow,
the violent altar

raised up at Golgotha,
our separating sin –
but bored by long sermons,
fazed beneath Massade's sun –

bread of the covenant
and cool thimble of grape

xiv
juice feed our hunger
until the service ends
and we go home. Wayside
cities of God from Anse

Cochon to Saltibus
gather these judges of
angels, heirs of Zion,
reluctant remnant, from

Caesar's plantations, a
ransomed Commonwealth.

89

xv

Come ye disconsolate!
Shake your places underneath
the golden menorahs
of mango blossoms with

joy for the tumbling white
star of flowering coffee,
soft settling lilac
of cedar, morning-glory's

royal purple heart, these
signalling witnesses

xvi

to the emptying tomb.
Holy convocation,
sing to the LORD new songs
on violon, chak-chak

and drum. Dance a measured
weedova you daughters
of David, around
the folded vacancy

of the ark's hollow linens,
its torn rock-stone veil.

xvii

At these borders of faith,
poems appear as canticles,
sketches shape to icons,
fireflies play the oracle

in a garden that calls
its roots Mahanaim — camp
of God — and like famous
cities we've never come

to, Christ's Road and Kingdom
grow more familiar with

xviii
each love that inhabits
now only fractured scenes
of dream and memory.
The age grows gross with sins,

stupidities of sons,
poutings of illiterates,
useless parliaments —
everywhere these failed states

of men disintegrate
to shameless anarchies.

xix
Ah Immanuel, clouds
are mantling Morne Gimie's
peaks in their rehearsal
of that Easter coming

when You arise, naming
Your elect, calling all
Your friends to gather
on the heights with angels,

in the unfathomable
arms of God's embracing

xx

mystery. From Silver Point
we contemplate that first
sight of You, dear Lord Christ:
You are laughing my fears

away O Father, Your Face :
effulgent Joy : Eyes : trans-
forming my reflection,
and at last : in Your uni-

maginably kind Hands :
our crowns of righteousness.

xxi

The shift of slipping art
invites our framing hearts
to sketch now His hedge of
grace encompassing us –

surf lace waking those mornes
to benediction, hill
lamps that make grateful psalms
from darkening Atlantic,

such poems that draw us, and
invite His grace extending.

ELEMENTAL

(for John Figueroa)

"But thou art gone, and thy strict lawes will be
Too hard for libertines in Poetrie."— Thomas Carew

1. air

In the blue-dyed surfing of air
an inverted rainbowl
perches its prismatic lips
across the gracious, steadfast earth,

and in Veronica's garden
a cavorting butterfly prevaricates
among the vanes
of pigeon-peas' yellow blossoms,

and across town,
you yearn after those sexy dancers
barrelling through space,
arching, escalating over breath.

Contemplating Morne Gimie's triple mornes,
I envision Him
taken from our clouding sight,
upon the elevating air.

2. earth

This schismatic aeroplanet, earth,
lithosphere soaked in dew –
>the gazetteer indexes fire
>at the end of forest, herb,
>tuber and clay goblet.

In the geology, mark:
>the elemental shack
>the silicon ziggurat
>the encrypted shard
>the tabular chip
>the loaded tumbril
>the exploding capsule
>the nuclear arrowhead
>the bludgeoning stone.

Mark also, in Pliocene:
>the loping hominid –
>an Ancient Potter fired for Himself
>a fine mud-skin,
>a microlith of bone, and divers artefacts.

>After the wheel and turn,
>He applied the bellows.
>Behold your fossil!

Mark well, under tectonics:
>The Incarnating God.

3. fire

Coal-pots of Choiseul –
      vestal basins at the heart of these earth yards,
      adamantine petroglyph on the stone air,
      abstract mobile,
      faithful utensil defying obsolescence,
      (gift of Prometheus the Potter?).

Do I too not take the black syllables of charred root into my wide mouth,
eager pyromaniac of swamping obsessions,
and push hard draughts into that narrow funnel under those fat cheeks,
till the angry red ember erupts into raging tartar,
ravaging the slaughtered holocaust?

After, descent to the hollow bole of clay,
exile of flaming faith,
and gift laid in ash.

The Angel comes, they say,
with seven of these self-same braziers,
and the Fire of the Altar
waits to pour Himself a Kindling
on the tinder world.

4.   water

> Can water imagine itself
> in the fire-heart of light
> in the earth-mound of dark
> in the silver palimpsest of air?

Who is as spendthrift as water
as extravagant in posture –
> framing herself in the globular dew
> and the storm-charged surfeit
> of irrevocable mass of hefting river?

Who is as profligate as water
as dissolute in exhibition –
> abandoning herself to wanton mud-hole
> and the spreading obscenities
> of stagnant, outrageous sewers?

Who is as stable as water
as firm in place –
> flexing under the Feet
> that once strode across
> her heaving face?

> Start with an image of water –
> in the fire of erupting ends of days
> in the turquoise depth of earth's mornes
> in the blue-dyed surfing of air.

LINE
(for Derek Walcott at 75)

"The lines have fallen to me in pleasant places;
yes, I have a goodly heritage." — Psalm 16:6

i.

Within the boundaries of my mortgaged peace,
bordered by unruly ficus, some struggling croton,
forsaken fallen palms and other anonymous waste:

Veronica's scattered variety of roses, Simone's
sensible vegetables, Kamara's clump of scruffy cat-tails,
and, swimming in Babonneau air like a tentacled sea-anemone,

the breadfruit; only today, *"Jules' tree-trimming*
crew" from Desbarras sawed down the ant-infested mango. Among
other unknown pretty-flowered bush: from Joy's time,
the elegant Easter spider-lily, in all her seasonal fragrance.

ii.
"to every line there is a time and a season." (DW)

When have I not measured this land by your lines?
When have I not tracked blue-smoke pits to their river-stone roots by
your metaphor?
When have I not walked, Walcott, by your fire-scorched love, through
uptown lanes

of old Castries, strolled the revolving corners of Chaussée, Coral,
Broglie, Victoria?
You leave us your covenants with the everlasting fretworked eaves
of Riverside Road, gommier *canots* and their men from Dauphin
to Vieux Fort,

the epiphanic groves of Mon Repos, the stone chapel of Rivière Dorée,
the turning leaves'
whispering of Methodist hymnals on Chisel Street.
It's what's left, at the end of the line (I imagine you insisting) that
scans our lives,
marks our season's faith, and amortizes all indentured loans.

iii.
"qu'est-ce que la poésie, si elle mérite son sel,
sinon un langage qui passé de main en bouche?" (DW)

The cross-hatching drizzle imitates flaking snow.
It's not Boston, just Castries, near the Square.
Snow, or warm rain, whatever city, the sketchy common news

these days is of war in ancient lands, terror
in towns whose subways we've negotiated,
vice parading proud banners in new Gomorrahs.

And while the bellowing fog of Babel's collapsing ziggurats chokes
5th Avenue with the same old hatreds –
from some obscure archipelagic galaxy,
unknown nebulae, light-years ahead,
sign fresh canticles to patient watchers on Becune's surf-battered coast
and on hill-top hamlets of Plateau.

iv.
"but come, girl, get your raincoat, let's look for life
in some café behind tear-streaked windows..." (DW)

I didn't see any 36 views of Mount Fuji. From the bullet-train to Kyoto,
Fuji wasn't there for the film. Like Morne Gimie in July, forest worlds
floating in self-indulgent cloud.
I did see Kabuki – at a theatre near Ginza Station, on Harumi Street
in Tokyo –

language winged like pagodas, lines played for wood-block prints of
Tokaido
traffic, teahouse courtesans, bombastic actors. Didn't see Hiroshima. Or
Nagasaki.

Sound a gong, lay a blossom on the lily pond of the Golden Pavilion
– for Roddy,

Brodsky and André Tanker. For these gracious, courteous, transmigrated
souls, pour a rice saké
as you pass the Shinto shrine near your hotel. These lives line your work
as ours –
shoguns and faithful companions following some Minshall dragonfly
muse, from Gulag to Santa Cruz,
faith drawing our straggling band to this sepulchral escarpment – as in
some "View from Moule à Chique, after Hokusai." Or, after Apilo.

v.
"The only art left is the preparation of grace." (DW)

Did Blake see angels sitting in the neighbours' trees?
Did an angel smile at me on a train platform in cold Boston one Winter?
Will Christ come with Ezekiel's four-faced cherubim and their fiery
wheels?

In this dark networking age, the schoolmen assassinate the Author,
desecrate the groves of wonder,
scrabble on their bellies to find significance in the dung of scarabs; in
columns of sneers,
they sniff out apostasy, line-up heretics, trigger disputes. Orwell warned

us of those tenured tyrants. Come Virgil and Dante, Aesop and Pascal,
come griots and chantwèls, come Ti Jean and Anancy,
come, fireflies peeping from evening bush of Monchy, chase
'way those soucouyants!

We passing through Vanity Fair, learning our lines, Grace steering us,
to reach in front the Ancient of Days, Who sitting on the circle of the
created stratosphere.

vi.
"I am going down to the shallow edge to begin again,
Joseph, with a first line, with an old net, the same expedition." (DW)

After the largesse of Sweden – gold medal, hand-written scroll, krona
quickly gone in the exchange;
after the depth of the N circled on the Konserthuset carpet,

after the cramped hands weary of inscribing yet another title page –

did you sense the hound stirring to its feet
as you entered the Grand Hotel? Faithful guardian of the craft
that brought you here, he would not leave

his master to banquet whisperings of sirens, braided tongues of polite
laughter,
even generous cushions under his exhaustion. He points Pissaro's
island.
He scents Becune Bay. He is eager for the Bounty of futile
mutinies that fall as lilac cedar settling around the patient Hound.

vii.
Okay. Time for this procession to begin.
The legacy gathering. The Monsignor waiting in the appointed place.
M'sieu Kendel, take the chak-chak please. Call violon, bones and
mandolin.

Princess Jane, you carrying the Choiseul panier of petals. Majèstwa
Dixon, please
to bring your dear stentorian self. You leading this line.

Chantè Fish Alphonse, where you? The weedova dancers

ready?
                    — And now, if it please your floral majesties, King Derek and
                                         Queen Sesenne,
to grace us with your pleasantries — we must go up,
to bring our arts' offerings to the Son,
the First in line, the End of metaphor, the Psalm of the Embracing
                                         Voice...

HARBOUR LOG

(Castries, August 1955)
"Statio haud malefida carinis" (old Badge of St. Lucia)
"A safe anchorage for ships."

In Port yesterday:
Schooners: *Augustus B. Compton*,
Acadius, *Adalina*,
Columbia, *Enterprise*,
S. Enid, *Rebecca E. Mitchell*.
Steamer: *Electra*.
Sloop: *Lady Edwards*.
Motor Vessels: *Biscaya*, *Privateer*, *Nanin*, *Wanderer*.
Yacht: *Phenix*.

Arrivals:
Motor Vessel *Lady Stedfast*, 87 tons, under capt. L.A. Marks, from St.
Vincent, consigned to Peter & Co.

Departures:
Schooner *Grenville Lass* to Martinique.
Motor Vessel *Fernwood* to Barbados.

Expected:
Motor Vessel *Nina* on August 11.
H.M.S. *Burghead Bay* on August 24.

Meanwhile:
Sylvestre JnBaptiste, alias Master,
Seaman of Mary Ann Street, Castries,
was found guilty by the Magistrate in the First District Court,
on a charge of unlawfully assaulting and beating
Dorothy Drayton, Laundress of Brazil Street, Castries,
on July 23.

CANTICLES
For the Lord Jesus Christ

Creation praises
Contract
Volcano
Parade
Ikon
Kweyol Canticles
First Things
Temptations
Abel
Rain
Babel
The Passion Canticles
Canticles of the Risen Life
The Art of Faith Canticles

CREATION PRAISES

In cathedrals of palmistes
chapels of flamboyant
shrines of banana fronds
grottoes of cocoa
groves of ripening mango
sanctuaries of anthurium
holy places of fern,
praise the LORD.

O, cleanse this earth, O Lord,
from hypocrisies of spirit
cruelties of heart
idolatries of mind
envies of eye
seductions of palm
besetting vices of soul –
save, O Lord, the profligate root.

Hunchbacked egret
boldfaced grackle
scandalous pipirit
idling gull
prowling hawk
neurotic flowersucker
critical hen –
let every thing that have wings, praise the LORD.

I will sing unto the LORD
for Shabeene and Dougla
sweet eye and quick hip
gap tooth and full lip
long limb and smooth skin
beauty reluctant, grace divine –
and send you forth with blessings,
wayfarers of my heart.

105

CONTRACT

And turning some Castries corner so familiar I don't even notice it,
on some day so unremarkable I don't recall it cool or hot —
distracted then by some matter of expenditure or composition or
was it passing lust,
I won't remember which.
In any case, at leisure or in haste,
shall I turn the anonymous corner, on that day still to be lost,
to meet — the Lord Assassin — with my name in the barrel of his fist?

Forget the avatar. Forget the extras diving under sidewalk trays.
Today, your death will die. The Contract is paid. Selah.

VOLCANO

What were they like, the last days of those buried cities – Sodom,
                              Pompeii, St. Pierre –
before the breasts salted in sulphur, the scorched shards of precious
                              mosaic, the orphaned sea-side avenues,
before the scattered ruin of temples, and villas gone to charnel-houses?

Thoroughly modern destinations – the women glamorous and callous,
men corpulent in stampeding chariots, dance halls promiscuous,
all the talk of scandals, crime, pestilential beggars;

and poets neglected, prophets tolerated –

On the familiar morning skyline,
the throat of the volcano dissolves in descending cloud.

PARADE

After the promised irruption of heaven into earth
and subsequent looting of the enemy's barrows,
imagine – the astounded hurtling of hawk, the disconcerted wonder
of hen,
pup's amazement, astonished mule, kitten dumbfounded, pipirit
shocked!

And then, the heirs of God, cerement free, parading the blue air.

So great leviathan, cattle, creeping thing, each to its kind,
rise without burden, with the lords of the air,
to come to their City, and their names calling out,

from the Lamb's opening Book.

IKON

Now He bears the image of His mother:
all-infolding eyes, smile settling at the lips' corners,
the rest of the face profoundly patient —

her Root, her Offspring, her Overshadowing Conception,
her Magnificent Annunciation, her Spirit-ravished Passion —

pondering liturgical mysteries, oppressed by the banal and tyrannical,
the children borne by this Incarnation
wait expectant as the willing will.

KWÉYÒL CANTICLES

(for Patrick 'Paba' Anthony, priest and folklorist)

1.
Let us praise His Name with an opening lakonmèt
and in the graceful procession of weedova;
let laughing, madras-crowned girls rejoice before Him in the scottish
and flirtatious moolala, its violon hinting of heartache.
And while we forget time turning in quick-heeled polkas,
pause during the tentative norwegian –

for when the couples end the gwan won,
you alone must dance for Him your koutoumba.

2.
I was glad when they call me to go up in the Séwénal.

The violon scraping my heart,
banjo and kwatro thrumming my grief like their plectrum,
and the guitar pulling my heel.

– I only seeing her tuning the mandolin on her bosom –

Then the chakchak shake me loose, insisting, insisting,
"Wait for the bow, the bow and the courtesy,
wait for the sax, the drum and the kwadril to start." Selah.

3.
And so, she has come: to the gold-flecked Wob Dwiyèt,
its long train in folds over her left wrist,
the clean petticoat adorned with lace,
the satin foulard, the head-piece of rainbow madras —

from the nondescript costume of the far city,
from the profligate famine of Barnard's estates —

to the embracing plenitude of Kwadril chakchak and violon,
to that Bright Brooch on the glistening triangular foulard.

4.
The cascading words of my hand
pluck His praise from eight-string bandolin and local banjo,
place His favour on madras and foulard, the satin and the lace,
plant His steps in mazouk, lakonmèt and gwan won;
point His casual grace in yellow pumpkin star, pendular mango,
plait Him a crown of anthurium and fern —

He is the Crown, the Star of grace, the Dancer of creation,
the Robing of righteousness, Tuning of the spheres,
Hand of the Incarnating Word.

FIRST THINGS

Against that primordial abyss, Word and Light.

Space expands before Them.

Earth ascends to the borders of her seas, to seed herb and fruit.

For almanacs, calendars and clocks – the garnishment of astronomical heights.

Out of the waters – sea-birds, flying-fish and (some say) Dragon and Leviathan,

while, in desert, pasture and canyon, turn the worm, milk-cow and behemoth.

In the Mesopotamian Garden, King Man and his Woman name the bright-winged reptile coiling the fenced-off tree.

It is Sabbath night.

TEMPTATIONS

It is clear she was beguiled by the Serpent's sinuous flatteries.

But he, was he — seduced by her full-curving softnesses, allured by
those flittering
lashes — tripped into the parting chasms of her sweet flirtatious
mouth? (So says the old poet.)

Or, eavesdropping,
Curious Man, did he wonder about the Crystal Gate, the proffered
dominion,
the deadly enticements of wisdom?
Whichever, flouting the order, he chose.

Just one more query — those tunics of covering skin,
were those the first-born lambs they had loved above all others?

ABEL

"O my Father, Father of my father and my mother,
Keeper of the pastures of the heavens and the earth, my Keeper;
at the very end of days, receive the first-fruits of my prostrate loins,
and have regard to the offerings of my stretched-out joints;

O Father, my Father, the tiller of the ground
has ploughed the seed of my blood, out of the scattering gourd
of his cruel hands, into the reluctant mouth of the sorrowing earth;

O Keeper of my spirit, will Your Countenance not fall against such
sacrifice, so fugitive, so vagabond, so cursed?"

RAIN

We'll never see the sky again.

The sun is dead under that slate shroud roped to buried horizons.
And the water tearing off the roofs is not funny anymore.

The merchants' curses chase their bazaars down pouring thoroughfares.
Already, already, fretworked gables are clinging to their astounded
citizens.

From here (no Ararat, just a simple morne), under bedraggled cedars, I
see him gone,
my Shem, my gone Shem, pacing the breaking fountains of the deep in
his terrible barge —

and we, we and our proud bird-soaked hills, to the flushing of the vortex,
a drowned heap.

BABEL

Then we clambered down the mountains of the East into a plain
of Shinar.

By the river, we set our flocks, and our songs were one lip,
one pleasing.

But Nimrod, black and dread Cushite, against the elders,
cursing the curse, pitched the gate of his lion god, and baked brick for
the climbing tower of Marduk.

So the Lord God of Shem set confusion in our ears in that place,
and the splitting tongues of His fire scattered us far,
with utterance unspeakable.

Then I came to Ur,
the holy testaments of Eden stuttering under my scorched lips.

THE PASSION CANTICLES
(for Charles Cadet)

Prologue: The alabaster flask

Over the bowed Head, the anointing oil of nard
pours from Mary's broken alabaster flask —
certainly, she filled that room with the fragrant adoration of her Lord;
certainly, even then, some grudged Him that embalming, with
their indignant jealousy — you heard it in the thief's voice,
sneering at the poor;

and the Master, raising His burial, raising her memorial, raises
their approaching loss,
beyond the maddening fragrance of the pure
ointment. But the bedeviled thief rose in envy, and over Christ,
his bottled hatred broke.

Caiaphas

"Who is this, this peasant prophet, wailing shoah on the city?
What is this riot of rags and branches down the thoroughfare?
And why this bacchanal of blasphemy resurrecting from Bethany?
Which Balak sends this Balaam's foal to mock Messiah?

Where next this din of thieves, this unwashed brood of publicans?
Will they impale the merchants and the bankers and the priests
on their hosannas
when they've stormed the precincts of the porch?
While their ambitious carpenter withers, as usual, in some
forgotten Arimathean sepulchre?"

Berith

Bitter herbs, bread unleavened, wine, and lamb slain between the
two evenings –
do the twelve comprehend they are settling the last rites of
Exodus, sipping the
watered dregs of that final Pascha?
And beyond fiction, in the Servant's holy hands, the betraying
heel. And the flat-footed
denials. And the splayed doubts. And other such leavenings.

Out of the common dish comes the separating sop to deepen
their perplexity.

So there, above some obscure alley in His City, all our wretched
story – Eden, Sinai, Golgotha –
is passed over, for His Bread, His Wine, His bitter Tree.

Later still, such talk under the brooding night! Then prayer, a hymn,
and over the Kidron, into Gethsemane.

Gethsemane

What commenced in the other garden begins to end here,
in the shadow of an olive mill by a black brook.

"Behold, We have become like one of them, to bear
their sorrows and their griefs." Let the wheel break
this Fruit on every tooth and tread. Bruise
the Seed under the trampling heel of the Bull
of Bashan. Pour the sweating barrel
of this agony into the cupping palms of God.

"Ecce homo"

"O Galilean, robed in purple, crowned with thorns,
is this Your estate? Is this Your kingship,
reduced to the scourge of their envy and spit? God born
of man, behold Your truth: silver kisses treacherous palms, shape-shifters
rend their costumes at cock-crow, the Pavement is soiled
by the desolation of Your bloody Purity. Look Carpenter,
is Caesar not adored, is Barabbas not preferred?
See, Holy Fool, You and Your Jews, I wash my hands of You!"

Friday

They leave Him nothing but irreducible nakedness –
no fig-leaf girdle, no swaddling cloth, no seamless tunic;
they impale the battered Scarecrow on the Skull's brow; their final curses
perforate the darkening skin of the sun; His distending knuckles
claw the veil of the God-forsaken air; yet, even now,
He thirsts only for the sour wine at the end of the hyssop branch; stricken
between earth and heaven, His heart opens to a new covenant,
and pours its blood and water on the Father's reconciling Hands.

Epilogue: Piéta

"He was all scattered, empty-limbed, exhausted, gone,
when I gathered Him off the stake. O my Son,
my Son! I was more Your son than You were mine,
Your tentative disciple, peeping out the Council's shutters
for Your Kingdom.
O my wounded King! Holy, Holy, Holy Child!
O my dear, bruised Prince!

O Father, receive Him in our poor linen, swathing His torn
flesh. May these paltry spices herald His approach
to Heaven's Throne. O LORD, give this Your Servant rest
in Your eternal Rock."

CANTICLES OF THE RISEN LIFE
"I will awaken the dawn." – Psalm 57:8

Except

"Death is the end and the end is death" –

Except: for the folded linens at the end of the sepulchre.
Except: for my name rising against the morning's doubt.
Except: for the familiar footfall behind the bolted door.
And except: for His punctured Hand in mine.

O Life, Life, Life! – no hope more sure,
no faith more certain:

the end is Life and Life is the end.

Bloodfire!

I shall arise, singing, from the far city,
against bludgeons, ghetto guns, gangs of the merciless,
child stranglers, kidnappers of the old, abusers without pity,

against the vacuous bakanal, the denuding pornography, the damned noise;
and I shall chant against the dead politicos, the corrupting pastors,
the self-adoring artists, the capering pimps and their boys –

I, rising man, go call down the cantors
of Mount Zion to raise Jah's judgement on these cursing lands.

Risen Man

"Have you ever shaken hands with a man who was dead?
Have you ever looked into the laughing eyes of a man who beat death?
Have you ever sat next to such a one and shared his salt bread?
Friend, do you know the incomparable odiferousness of the breath
of a resurrected man? Friend, have you been led in Zion's psalms
by a voice that scattered the doomed wealth

of Satan's domains? Stranger, I have known the encompassing arms
of such entombing and embalming Grace."

Manifest

"Because every fruit is a gift rising from the eternal Seed
interred beyond the catacombs of exfoliating nebula,
encrypted in the woollen cerements folded like the ancient parchment
of a deed in the Hand of God, we sing this sedulous
faith. Handling such mysteries, probing parable and metaphor,
we arrived at this plain board (after the incredulous
hour) to find that urns of maize and grape had manifest
their witness into bread and wine. And fish."

Return of the prodigal

After the reggae hard-beat, the Haitian guitars and the delicate mazouk,
the unattainable sloe-eyed dancers, sips from forbidden chalices,
and the inevitable descent to the wood-and-zinc
shack – you came to count your losses,
exhume, with some embarrassment, his unread letters,
raise, to your startled heart, his shameless wishes –

then, giving up your feet and hands to love's caressing fetters,
you arrived again in the familiar yard, to the evening's last trumpet.

THE ART OF FAITH CANTICLES
(for Kwame Dawes)

Writing the ikon

You must now enter the silence alone and listen. Wait.
Wait for the translation of the first line. Write.
Write with your fingers searching the pigments on the palate
for the essential shading of the right
image. The medium frames the sacred intercession.
To give face, posture and voice to the holy is no trite
matter. And where humility unveils some gracious incarnation,
offer first this blessed sacrament to the King of saints.

Sacramental

"When I remember the angst-ridden sonnets and mincing couplets,
those self-regarding bit parts in pretentious existential dramas,
the coffee-and-cigarette nights of self-righteous zealotry –
it's not regret or shame that idly scrolls the names
of gone lovers and drifted days. I had lost faith in that circus
before I found myself in this office copying hours of psalms
(what more can paltry poetry say?) and signing pure colours
of sacred faces
across the illuminating columns of these holy books."

Palimpsest

On this scarred island palimpsest, the Master has etched His colophon.
It's the final engraving – after Sumerian clay and Nile papyri,
Macedonian vellum and Lindisfarne
illuminations; after the Dead Sea
parchments, the German incunabula, and all those versions
of His oracles –

in short, the transcripted history of The Book. We
must learn again the alphabet of Eden and Gethsemane's canticles,
and hope to read our names in His unfolding scroll.

Oracle

"It is not true that spirit is invisible. He proclaims himself in several guises:
astute aphorism, careless cliché, oracular jargon,
declamatory rhetoric, many-costumed metaphor, multiple voices.
Look for the ring of truth, the thumbprint of conviction,
the image of reflection, the turning line.
There is a Voice that speaks beyond incomprehension.
Read faces carefully for the plain
speech of an Artisan who builds tables and universes."

Canticle

After poems, psalms. And canticles of island pilgrims
passing through self-important harbours, smoke-blue banana valleys,
villages lounging at the curves of bougainvillea lanes. Faith limns
your life salted by Atlantic trades, fretting with Creole violons,
the children gone to hard rock malls of Kingston and Flatbush.

O – in the beloved corner shrines of mango blossom, breadfruit palm,
almonds' broad oval
leaf, the chapels of sidewalks' hasty awnings, the confessionals of
indignant minivans, the
fuming censer of the streets' sulphur speech –

O, at every wary block – His Real Presence, and archangels
gossiping of His parousia. After
poems, psalms. And your canticles.

FLIRTATIONS

1.

Stranger, what is it that searches me as I probe my interest in you?
You deflect my gaze, shy out of my tentative fingers, embarrass me
                              as you turn, offended.
You leave no room to move — face shut, dead-ended.

Lately, however, I sense you yield,
calculating perhaps the profit in less defence,
swinging to a more open stance,

carefully indiscreet, without subtlety, without irony. Your
shallowness — is it? Your seeming illiterate-simple — is it affectation?
Are you dangerous? Does a viper dance

in that fattening body which allures beyond reason, beyond plain truth?
Am I making too much of nothing but self-indulgence
amused by my flattering flirtation?

2.

Can I trust you? With my — what?
With my angling protestations, my mid-life confusions?
With what confessions?

Will you misunderstand? Or understand too well?
And see through the old man's fumbling contradictions?
"What does he *want*?"

Affection settles warily
like a pup unsure of the hand's intention.

3.
It's like a weird dance
this circling of souls
signalling for a chance
to momentarily hold

some intimate instant
of naked recognition
beyond dead-end lust,
to *see,* in willing accommodation

the unencumbered *we.*

4.
Do they even think about it?
After all these years – the same flatteries,
the pinches in the same place
the eyes still teasing out

reproach, the smile gentle-tender.

That infinitesimal extra moment of goodbye
through the finger-tips still worries *why?*

PHOTOSNAP

In the photograph she stands well braced
in the doorway of the shack: her back is placed

upright firm against one frame, the left arm reaches across the
open door
to hold the other frame. Standing as she does, her feet are wedged
on the floor's

corner in front of her. That left arm, those locked feet, that braced
back,
block the entrance. He is more relaxed: facing her, no lack

of confidence, outside the shop, left elbow on the window sill,
right leg nearer us, rod-firm, left leg angled at the knee toward her;
the sharp felt hat fills

his profile with shadow, so we don't have a face; a fruit in his hands. So,
Mam, why so firmly angled? Your posture is saying *no*

entry, but aren't you (unsmiling, holding tight on the door jambs,
anchoring the open door at your back, securing the white painted
borders) praying hard against those well-suited charms –

and the sign painted above your head on the shack concurs –

"GOD PROMISE TO HELP"?

SPHINXE

Don't be distracted by the parted thighs
the elbow folding in a model's pose
the casual chemise and slipping skirt –

do you dare to enter the navel of her world
the enigmatic neither come nor go of her watching
your every moving thought,

to know her tracks and valleys and gardens
and coal-pits, her songs and secret places
her white yam and salt fish

and all the rest of her life in Babonneau hamlets,
that this alluring sphinxe
now guards?

MID-DECEMBER, MID-AFTERNOON

On the radio, classical music from horizon-clear Martinique.

Mid-December, mid-afternoon, light breezes under the over-
                    spreading mango,
across envined palmiste, through the abandoned garden, and you
                    imagine the shadows
lacquered, set. The antique
stone staircase, reduced to one forlorn curve and a few broken flagstones,
leans against the shade. In the frame, between grasses, is that an egret?
Pastoral pauses at Mount Pleasant, above Castries, in sight
                    of Morne du Don villas, high palms edging
the drift of hill across its barricade
of blue bent space.
                    Barack Obama,
certain strained friendships, the graduation of apprentices,
afternoon softening to pastel, numinous,
over Choc's procession of bright stones – what urgent
apocalypse hesitates to interrupt the coralita flirting among golden
                    crotons?

On the radio, creole music of Malavoi from Martinique.

INCARNATION

(for Vladimir Lucien)
— Hebrews 2:14

Out of the creeping undergrowth of manuscripts
words line themselves with the body of the page
immaculately. Leaving decorated margins
of our modest codex, we ache to glimpse the enraptured
end of the art of faith. In the font's innocent concavities
we imagine bold faces of eager messengers.
At the edge of improbable translation, we are assuaged
by incredible epiphanies cradling

in paperback covers.
                    Herod's night raiders read
Bethlehem right. The local chapter of Moloch
plots the setting of the star. Mythology
parses into facts: angels, shepherds, feeding trough –
where, in this part of the prologue,
the Death Defeater's mother laughs His gurgles to the kneeling kings.

SOUNDTRACK – 2010 A.D.

"out in the streets, they call it murder" (Damian Marley)

1.   *time, baby, circling*

time, baby, circling
artefacts of a near life
drawing a slip-knot

noose on the narrowing
midriff of the hourglass
harrowing our present griefs

like the persistent silt
of persistent floodings
of vexed rivers and collapsing mornes

cutting us off, compacting
all the now we have
into that new abyss at Colombette

that empty verandah in Summersdale
a vacant chair at Choc
and other washings-away

time, baby, circling
the precious artefacts
of our near lives

and the unrelenting slaughter –

baby in her cot
mother at her doormouth
Vanita Mirpuri over her cash register

LaBorde in his bed
the lovers on the beach
burned in their car

and so on, unrelenting slaughter
blood clotting over sidewalks –
and the unrelenting

irrevocable anger of furious brown waters
cannonading off broken landsides
choking over damned garbage

pushing rivers to riot
against flimsy barricades,
roaring, devouring roots of hills

– "unclean, unclean, unclean
too much blood in cracks of concrete
along swollen arteries of narrow yards

on the cruel hands of cursing Cains!" –
howling with the punching wind
in vain, in vain, in vain

against the punctured lungs
the axed skull, the shattered breastbone
the slaughtering of the girl Verlinda –

and desperate floods vomit their ochre hearts into the circling sea.

And will the sea not clamour
with her gathered brown relative
with the tectonic anger of her deeps –

against bloody bandits
and their accessories,
gangs of divided tongues, those serpents,

beasts without heart in fancy chariots
barons of death behind the scenes
brigands who defile the land with their deals –

and will the sea not raise a mighty tsunami
to purge the haunts of blood, blood, blood
too much blood on the innocent face of earth?

So, faith is certain of tomorrow's epiphany
but how to meet the apocalyptic moment of now
under fallen colonnades of the Presidential palace

tent cities of cholera and rape and empty-bellied children
the recurring decimation of mud in the kitchen
friends going to dementia, decrepitude and tumours,

and in honest mirrors, the apparent dysfunctions,
slipping names, insomnia, gathering pill boxes
and out of reach, envied flirtations with perfect lips,

sloe eyes and teasing hips. Add inescapable
anxieties, dead-end jobs that pay bills,
no prizes, no awards, the country grown strange and foreign

citizens mocking the devalued currency of art –
so, how to meet the apocalyptic hour
though faith is certain of the promised parousia?

2.   January 12th 2010, Haiti

i.   Madonna of Port-au-Prince

You who look like Alice
Your eyes red with shattered plaster and weeping
Your full lips bruised with dirt
Your hairpiece of locks slipping back like a cowl
The powder dusting your oval cheeks is grey concrete –
If the rest of you was not buried under rocks of blasted wall
And the figure in the foreground was not blood splattered
And someone's leg was not trapped behind you,
You could have been a pretty girl
With sand on your bare arms
Writing your name on a shell
On some beach off Les Cayes –
You who look like Alice
Another lost girl I used to know,
Not an ikon's model
On a chapel wall in Jacmel
But a strange Madonna anyhow
Flat on the scattered masonry
Sans enfant, or enfant gone from your hands
To the devouring earth –
The ikon herself
Impassive Erzulie, gazing through your Carib face
From a palette of pixels
Framing now before me.

ii. Maman

Did you find him, maman, the old man,
Or was it the grandchild left in your care for the day,
Or, in the catastrophe behind you,
The daughter who was setting your supper,
Or perhaps your friend, having a Dominican *ponche* with you?
Your long arms, maman, are bathed in the white dust of disastrous
                                        city-fall,
Your fingers are exhausted from their frantic and futile search for bones,
For hair, for a belt or a bodice,
For a baby, a baby who was impossibly there,
Gurgling at her spoon
Teasing your heart,
And you singing a lullaby, *"Haiti Cherie"*
Haiti beloved, beloved child,
Gone child, gone with the walls, the debris, the *tranblanterre*
                                        and the *lavalas*,
Gone from your arms, from your keening, scrabbling fingers
Despairing under block, under board, under broken back
And the child *disparu*, taken –
Or was it your friend from Cap Haitien,
Or the daughter who shared your name,
Or the old man – companion of your days,
Comrade of sleepless hours, keeper of your young heart
Comforter of those fallen breasts
Fallen under your torn chemise
Fallen with the roofs and the windows and the President's house
Fallen with the broken routes of Port-au-Prince
Fallen and forlorn, *Haiti Cherie*?

iii. Cathedral

The ionic columns hold nothing up
Not the twin cupolas that welcomed mariners to Port-au-Prince
Not the grand round windows of stained-glass ikons
Not the novenas of those who died in the fallen girders,
Unless you count the blue dome of vacant air
The ruined, ruined facades
The hovering stench –
Has Boukman triumphed?
Do Legba and Ghede aka Baron Samedi mount the buried altars?
Does Ogoun lie entombed in this broken peristyle?
Do these curious questions matter to the houngan
Crying down the mess of fallen masonry
To touch his daughter's ears? –

Outside the shattered cathedral
The women kneeling in the dust
Raise rosaries to the familiar Haitian sky
And lift their psalms
Past the ionic columns
That hold nothing up.

iv. At Capernaum, boats

"The people who sat in darkness have seen a great light, and upon those who sat in the region and shadow of death, light has dawned." – Matthew 4:16

This, the Port of the boat people
This, the Port of their Prince
Home-harbour safe
Docks of sails in sunset –
This is the Port of the boat people
After Dessalines and Duvalier, HIV and cholera
After tornado and tremblor
The Gadarene adventure and their Bay of Pigs
Canoewrecks off Florida, the invading boots of marines
From caravel to carrier –
After the desolate cities of my pilgrimage
And diverse tribulations
From deserts and catacombs to creole favelas,
These crosses of masts under the purpling evening
Their sails folding like seamless robes
The people neither coming nor going
Home-harbour safe
Intransit to the undying lands of their Prince
Who loved fishermen
Who slept in their boats
Roped their storms to His peace
And encompassed their little faith
With His incomprehensible love
Home harbour safe –
At Capernaum, boats
The Port of the boat people
The Port of our Prince.

v. In Caravaggio's ikon

In Caravaggio's ikon of Thomas seeing Christ
all eyes are locked to the doubter's firm finger
poking around the torn flesh, under

the strong hand of the Carpenter. Thomas,
Apostle to our secular, mocking, murderous
new age, meeting his worst-case scenario

with the firm grit of flesh under his thumb
that index of incarnation – incarnation, Immanuel
God is with us – under the impossible rubble

as we claw at the unimaginable earthfall, Immanuel –
over the body of someone's son fallen in crossfire
in shrieking shadowlands of betrayal

through terminal disorientation of disease, Immanuel.
Because that wound is real, the death was certain
here, beyond reason, beyond the apocalypse

of private disasters, is something else
is Life beyond life, beyond heartbreak
beyond assassination, beyond the tremblor

at three in the afternoon, beyond the amnesiac cancer of the mind.
Here, under our finger, is faith, here is hope,
and He asks us, against the brutal heel on the locked door

the harsh fist of imploding earth
the shroud covered bier –
"Love one another."

vi. Basket of prayers: A hymn of offering to God

My heart, O God, my heart
Enters now the Holy Place,
Where You wait with open arms
To meet me face to face.

My heart, O Lord, my eager heart
Bows low before Your Throne,
And trembles Lord to hear You start
To speak to me alone.

My heart, O God, my grateful heart
I offer now to You
A basket of my prayers;
To You beloved Lord,
A basket full of tears
That You alone have wiped away;
A basket full of fears
That You alone have cast afar;
A basket full of hurts
That You alone have healed;
A basket full of hope
That You alone have blessed me with;
A basket full of joy
That Calvary earned for me;
A basket full of prayers,
A basket full of prayers,
A basket, Lord, that's full of praise,
A basket Lord, that's full of praise,
My heart, O Lord, I give to You,
A basket full of praise.

"MY HEART HOLDS ROOMS"

My heart holds rooms I've never entered
doors concealed, secret entrances
sudden corners turning to knobs without keys –
Oh, some chambers I know familiar
favourite window seats, corner desks, comfort stations
boudoirs of great pleasure
and sacred crypts, twilight zones, forbidding cells
dread dungeons deep under dreams –

I've also danced and flown through octagonal halls, their slanting light
and played the cantor down glass staircases –

but those other places, the guessed at
the undiscovered, the unexplored
the mysteries of the curious heart –
are they the promised portals
to the mansions of His Father's House?

SPIRAL

for Pat C. – in memory

we return, never the same point,
that's gone, that's passed

but a familiar conjunction,
place, person, angled commemoration

unsettling déjà vu –
          from the hours' spiralling edge, I call you

to mind, to heart, to touch ghosts
in the stairwell, serious roots thrusting

us around today, tomorrow
to come here again yesterday, another furrow

another spiral turning up the past.

POEMS OF COPIAPÓ.

for Kamau Brathwaite

Wheel

Wheel, wooden support, winching cable
tradesman's materials of this miracle
in the desert of Copiapó,
like bread, like fish, like rain water turning to wine –
O wheel that lifts with inexorable, monotonous love
they that had gone, had sunk from sight, had disappeared
from hands that now hungered in regret,
eyes desperate for one more looking,
like the lovers of Port au Prince, the mothers of Medellin –
you are not the UFO some saw in 1864 over Copiapó
spectacular, a mythical Samsara
an Ezekiel fantasy of cycling whirlwinds,
but here, clamped above the blue cavern that entombs the 33
yoked to the capsule that falls relentlessly through the needle of a shaft
you return them each to terrible glory,
to impossible hope, from abysses of faith,
like Lazarus to the salt bread and green tea of his incredulous friends.

Last man out

"...and if the earth jolted now
or the weary cable shredded
or they forgot to count
the last fool embedded

in his damned courage
or the capsule door
opened up to wedge
that treacherous corridor

142

and has the weather changed
above the Atacama
and if the earth rearranged
now this blue tabernacle
and is she faithful
Cortella, Cortella —

O rod and staff me as You will
in the depths of this desert valley

as my soul waits
for the sound of the wheel
for the grate of the weary winch
for my portion of miracle

last one to be raised
'estamos bien en el refugio'
my soul waits
and in Your wheel I hope."

Supper at Copiapó

O blessed yard of chickens and cavorting pups
after that catacomb's dread and aborted hopes

and holy be the avocado blossoms of this precious plot
that will never lie in that grim grotto

and happy be the sacred rags of these grandchildren
whose prayers, I swear, will never wash the belly of that cavern

and how complete the worn hands of my old lover
that caressed my dreams at the end of the shaft of San José —

so, hallowed be this coffee cup, this corn, this wine
these companions of the gloom from day one to sixty-nine
that Your ineffable grace uplifted from Copiapó mine.

In October 2010, 33 miners who had been trapped underground in a mining disaster in Copiapò, Chile, were all rescued after 69 days.

"WILL LOVE HOLD"

After a photo by Vladimir Lucien

Will love hold, tight-roped between tears
certain of storm, not wanting loss

howling to horizon's abyss, heaving from despair?
Will love hold, memoried to casual harbours?

    And we were happy for a while, and forgot
    tomorrow coming, and coordinates we couldn't share.

Will love hold, when all is broken
and merciful tides of amnesia
cradle us till we wake?

AFTER GARY BUTTE

"So crossing the river
and walking the path
we came at last to Kumasi." — Kamau Brathwaite

Prologue: The merchant

Did he arrive at sunset's orange hour
or with the anonymous midday bustle
markets busy before Sabbath —
and evening or noon height, him,
stranger with strange wares
looking for a berth
in the fabled city.

Who wants cantos from placards of bewildered widows?
Totems to soft bones of decimated embryos?
Androgynous puppets parading obscenely between certain jars?
    — "Any credit for dark sayings of Babylon, Bhutan or islands
                    of the sea?"

Fifth Avenue needs no merchandise of prophets —
    with their Greek vases
    their silicon tablets
    their first editions
    high-speed subways and twin towers —
won't spare a dime for this third world primitive
his ark of Mesopotamian innocence
his naive style.

i. The way up

From Ur to Haran down the Crescent Valley to Egypt
back again to the terebinth trees of Mamre,
and the Canaanite was then in the land.
The Man came in the heat of the day
on their way to the boulevards and museums
the malls and stadia, suburbs and ghettos
to strange women and rich men's catamites.

After, the plain of Siddim smoked like a cursed holocaust
and salt pillars lined the road to Zoar.

ii. The new age

> *"city of gold,*
> *paved with silver,*
> *ivory altars, tables of horn,"* — Kamau Brathwaite

remembrances of ghosts:
masks of indifferent hostility
nightmares we had not imagined
shame applauded across networks
distractions at the frenetic tips of fingers —
             privacy, thought, prayer
                  'itation, Jah —
                         banished.

iii. A kiss

"It was the bolero, Ramona, the bolero,
a kiss of jazz creole
lady with the Rita Dove lips,
not forgetting Maritza,
Andean pan flutes breathing reggae
at El Solar Casa Cultural in Bucaramanga –
Celia Cruz, Lady Day, Sesenne Descartes,
Piaf, Edith Lefel, Makeba,
souls many, so many, Ramona –
lovers scarved with rainbows
scattering galaxies out of sad earth
raising for us pardons, benedictions, homecomings."

iv. Doors to infinity

Turnstiles, tokens, trains
eternity of rails receding

Flirtatious oval eyes
retreating to masques of faces

The familiar loved
becoming stranger

You between the glass doors
echoing reflections

Your heart, furtive,
fervent, fugitive.

v. Animal man to angel

> *"the sons of God saw the daughters of men that they were fair;*
> *and they took them wives of all which they chose"* — Genesis 6:2

In the chronicles of giants
Fire loved a woman of earth
with peacocks at her feet
hibiscus through her locks
and deep dimples under her laughing —

When she betrayed him
(his fantasies bored her eventually)
for a one-boat fisherman and his spectacular nets
flung over green islands
and flying fish,

their son, confused between his elements,
took to the airwaves
and broadcast himself Hurucán
furious against surf, hill,
defiant lamp.

Epilogue: Morning roosters

> *"and the feather, red*
> *rooster, reminds us he*
> *watches;" — Kamau Brathwaite*

A rumour, and more than a rumour, of cockerels —
from Kumasi to tents of Kedar
from markets of Sichuan
to Port of Spain's Savannah —

The great Comb that raised the world to the first sun
comes again with His plumes and spurs
comes to take for Himself a harem of a bride
from every coop and hen house of earth

Egyptian Fayoumis, Japanese Bantams,
Rhode Island Reds and Blue Cochins
Guinea Hens and Creole Leghorns,
among the bridal caravan of pullets —

He comes of course, with morning
and trumpet radiance of the last sun.

FOR SEAMUS HEANEY 1939-2013

i.
"Places of writing" — Sandymount Strand to Becune Point
by way of Mossbawn and Chaussée Road
then to Choc and Bellaghy — our corners and yours

where hens squawk under guava trees
and I imagine furrows of Derry in Autumn mists
the blackbird frantic on the skylight of Glanmore —

and Creole violons you loved with their ancient men
are gathering on Walcott's surf-splattered verandah
with remembrances of you in *lakonmèt* and *moolala*

and always, always, joynoise of poets, chak-chak players
tuned with our poteen. Ah Seamus!
We strike our notes and dig to roots of ploughs.

ii.
"Noli timere," fear not, as we open the roof of clods
and let him down the mosswalls of Bellaghy
among the scattered cloths and beds

of poets, prophets and men of the palsy
who fall to Compassion in the hammocks of Love
and rise and walk in the grace of Mercy

gratefully.
Harmonies of harps and violons lift above
Carrauntoohil and Morne Gimie, Castle Dawson and Castries.

A CITY AFFAIR

(for the St. Lucian poets)

"Don't you know I love you but am hopeless
at fixing the rain?" — Derek Walcott

We meet on the bus stand
our affair hidden in shouldering crowds –
another Wednesday, memory scouting through old Castries
retrieving lost facades, missing bars, gone tailor shops,
among sidewalk bazaars,
Syrian emporia, pastel food-huts
and aloof *desmoiselles*.

Full disclosure –
no affair, just some aging poet's fantasy
of a shapely muse from Marc or Millet
gentle spirit dissing corny flirtations
with watchful eyes and dimpled chin.

I guess our island cities age with us –
too-familiar corners turn weary with worn paint
houses that once welcomed you lean into broken steps
grime has grown dirty grey at the head of certain streets
we have become old strangers with the stranded shoemaker
near Victoria and Chisel.

Alert for bag snatchers and stray bullets,
pressing against all that life
in the anonymous teeming of this culture –
what do we love, if we love, and how doubt that we love?

        : brash illiterate glamour, gossip of salons and parlours,
incomprehensible jabber of Jamaican Gaza from young pirates' trays,
70's chic thickened into retirement and resignation;
those around the park who recall

what we have forgotten about ourselves –
how doubt that we love the faithful harbour
closing in twilight after the cruisers,
soft-candle light settling from Mount Pleasant to Morne du Don to
Morne Fortune
sudden scattering of fine drizzle,
remembrances of yards, rooms, first loves
and evenings coming down to town –

And I see I have gone to fictions of memory
asking of love now
as a man searches the warm ashes of a long marriage
to find again, if he can, the first coal,
glowing infatuation,
and under inquisition to seek out
what do we love, if we love and how doubt that we love?

On quiet Wednesdays, in lanes and streets of old Castries
passing through bus stands
looking, I suppose, some epiphany –
I imagine apocalypse
the last muted trumpet coming up
under that strange harmony of voices, sound-systems, traffic.

And O, I fear, I yearn, I hope,
for these I do love,
how doubt that I love,
beyond my heart's flooding boulevard –

for these
I plead, I pray, O Christ
Your enrapturing Grace.

CITY REMEMBRANCES

i. Song for Gaboo, music man 1948-2014

You were our first star
maestro of Broglie Street
your piano flourishes cascading down the evening –
and all those escapades
all those capsules of remembrances
turning up childhood sidewalks;

the old school room is still there, greening
near the square belfry and same dilapidated cemetery;
wise ghosts of our teachers
are scouting the yard for you,
you, re-arranging their overtures,
playing down the tracks,
skanking your own riddim.

Why does news of your death surprise me, music man,
surprise me with my love for you
my first star, *my-mate,*
Gabriel Mondesir?

ii. For McDonald Dixon at 70

"As we grow old, Impossibles shape before our eyes" (Dixon)

I must imagine you now
walking away
towards the waterfront
and vendors' arcade
turning, out of my sight, down Jeremie Street.

Come back, like a rewinding video
pedalling backwards
past our grey names
past yesterday's yesterday;
come with your sketches
come with your tattered manuscripts
come find some lost almond shade
up Vigie beach,

and let me learn from you
such faithful industry
beyond talent, beyond award
beyond tomorrow's tomorrow,

such faith that would hold my faith
steady, steady,
beyond our endings' never-ending line.

iii. Sabbathing Wednesday (for K.H.)

Yes, I would Sabbath Wednesday
proclaim procession through old parts of town
place shrines of palm booths under verandahs' ancient fretwork
and players of instruments at random corners;

mid-morning, mid-morning, a gentle air abroad,
benevolence at shop-fronts and half-opened jalousies,
angels ascending from Mary Ann to Broglie to Coral Street.

Yes, Wednesday for Sabbath,
resting centre of the week
pivot of our circling, cycling, repetitious livings;
but along the first sidewalks we skipped,
near those same zinc gates to alleys, yards and wooden steps
                              we recollect,
window ledges from which such courtesies and wisdom flowed –

to these our pilgrim feet should wander
with music up the road
away from downtown frenzy, frenetic sirens, hustlers,

on mid-morning Wednesdays,
Sabbathing.

FOR KAMAU BRATHWAITE AT 85

"Where are the open spaces now
clear sky, the stars, horizons' distances?"
— KB "The Forest" in *Masks*

We looked with you, pathfinder
into great halls, high spheres
of the seven kingdoms,

and you sang our lives
to memory
before the Golden Stool was lost
when we had our names
and names of the gods

and wombs of strong trees
were oracles under the skin of our hands.
From islands' scorned syllables
your horn lifted nations' new tongues

Castries to Kingston
Brixton to Brooklyn
Axum to Kumasi

as they now are. And it
it is now
now the Times of Salt

the age of griots archived
their heads hung in dark corners
their songs obsolete as vinyl

while ballheads of Babylon
deconstruct themselves
over abysses of mockery;

but children
who have not genuflected to Baal
who have remembered again

whom you name from the drum-
beating of your love
come, come, come

with oil of coconut,
bread of cassava, gooseberry wine,
tablets of fruit of your word, *Kamau.*

CANTICLES FOR DUNSTAN ST. OMER
1927-2015

Apilo, you set our liturgies to soar
from high vaults, domes and altarpieces
Castries, Monchy, Fond St. Jacques, Roseau

gave us voice to lift His praises
on tambou, chak-chak and trumpet conch
chantwèl and débot dancers in the procession of priests

tout manmay Kwéyòl, a first communion –
        a confirmation, He loves us as we are, our Flower King.

Before He was Madonna's, He was the Father's Son
The Word, begotten beyond comprehension –
look close within the Virgin's cowl in your ikon

Child reaching to mother, Abba embracing the Beloved,
mystery Incarnation, blessèd Fruit of the hallowed
Eternal Womb. Down to earth, He lived

like you, paint on His hands, among farmers and fishermen
raising them to Himself – Wonderful, Immanuel.

The man himself, you ask? –
See the grey-eyed rebel
from Castries CDC housing

in wry amusement under doctoral
cape, dead empire's tapping sabre,
papacy's golden medal;

loping with irrevocable confidence, sober
faith, flirtatious grin, about

the streets and shortcuts of his city
sharing love and peace with brother beggar
and young sister Ras – such gentle, easy benediction,

Saint Omer, actor, editor, tennis player and flag-maker –
the man, you say? – no time for lackeys, party charlatans
or the whitening history he painted black

on altar wall and road mural, under celebrating
laughter of simple towns and hamlets where his easel rooted.

"Heaven," says Derek, "is the place where painters go,"
so there you are, about your holy business
palette amazing, infinitude of canvases, your arrogance

beatified in His Light; it's not finished, seeing
further and deeper, scaffolding under the dome's back,
Ad Gloriam Dei, the making, the making,

Michaelangelo, Giotto, Caravaggio, Apilo
O Paradiso!

INTIMATIONS

i.
We step to eternity from now
the instant at our feet
the present intersection
of irrevocable hours —

what heart's door slams shut?
what terrible holy turns inside out?
what mirror fixes this corrupt?
what unbeing dislocates the shrieking ghost?

Ah, but blessèd saint,
clocks stilled and maps scrolled —

what high gates dissolve?
what holy tender comes?
what grace returns what grace?
what glory now unfolds within this earth?

ii. They

"*They all lie in wait for blood;*
Every man hunts his brother with a net." — Micah7:2

It's generosity that's not there.
They don't give, they distrust the open hand.
Their own worth is hidden from them.
Those bodies breed monster hearts.
They don't know their own beauty.
They don't trust love.
They don't love.
They don't.
They.

iii. Haiku

Camilo and me
cavorting in the shadows'
imagination

of their framed portraits
of Camilo and me, at
the surf-breaking end

of Ocean Spray, like
kindred spirits of shadows
of clouds on reef pools.

iv.

A woman who has loved me for fifty years is dying.
Weak, losing weight, she is terrified, denying.

I text every day, to say I am praying
for her, send Bible verses; I avoid prying

out diagnoses; she is private like that
and I have not been calling to chat.

What can I really say? I regret
her love was unrequited?

I was always touch and go
while you waited so

patiently for me to turn
to turn to you, to learn,

foolish boy, that you loved me
since 1965, that dinner party

where we first met? But why this line
when she is desperate for tomorrow alone,

back to normal, flirtations on the phone
complaints about the youth and her son's

self-willed ways? I should call,
speak of the weather and all

the flooding in town, talk of old
Castries and archived evenings unfolding

on Mary Ann Street, gripe
about politics, and grope

for half-imagined intimacies
with a joke. She wants life, fantasies

of what might have been, good remembrances
of yesterday, so she might delete today's encumbrances

of cancer's relentless gouging of her gut.

v.   1 Kings 1:1-4

And then there is Abishag
who cherishes the king –
he won't touch her when she bathes
him with bay leaves, singing
his psalms or teasing
with tent refrains
on the queen and that old affair;
he won't touch her full breasts
full under the wet blouse
and her hips clinging
to the soaked skirt and one mischievous
bay leaf on the tremulous curve of the world –
he won't look when he stands in the tub,
shaking with cold in his bones
desiring in his blood
as she towels him with wool from Lebanon –
later, he won't interfere with her
when they sleep on each other
and she warms him with her hot body
under the quilted Shunammite coverlet –
Abishag, the tender.

vi.

"The Spirit of the LORD spoke by me, And His word was on my tongue." —
2 Samuel 23:2

      "Ah, Holy Spirit,
how could I have scrolled such mighty things
if You, Cantor of heaven
had not breathed your sweet psalms
upon my stubborn head;
      hearing inside hearing
seeing without seeing
chapters of apocalypse,
leaving Your Word, its precise
prophetic utterance;
      send Lord, my cloak from Troas
the books of the old poets
the Salt Sea parchments
the family engravings from Tarsus;
      that shaky knee hates the cold
I need some more ink
this vellum is caked with mould
I think too much of the pancakes
of Prisca in Corinth;
      the centurion grumbled to himself
but I heard without hearing
soon it comes, soon it comes
the black hood bearing
the clean-edged knife
      block under my chin
last squawking chicken
outside the door, last mouse
scurrying in the straw, the last damp house.
      Ah Holy Cantor, even so, even so..."

vii.   *after Melissa Green*

The applause of city lights, casual coffees in bookshops
packed, sleek auditoriums and you at the rostrum,
coveted blurbs sign your beautiful editions –
                              comes the grey heron
through your eyes, its low, swift slide to the wet sand
and the irrevocable, eternal end of surf, tumbling.

Continents under rails and routes of your camaraderie
argot of champions skirting sink-holes of envy
exuberant joy in the gossiping of friends –
                              soughing casuarinas
murmuring wood-doves, alarum of the red-breasted scissor-tail
over a rumour of sharks, pretend to fill the silence of their absence.

Encroaching decrepitude, terrifying occasional amnesia
lungs and heart lurching to wheeze and raking cough
paranoid insomniac –
                              like sleep it comes when it comes, and though
as in dreams, you are here but there, so like a trip to Boston
you will be there, really there, dreaming here, on some unutterable
                              artery of a thoroughfare.

viii.

"chayé mwen avan syèl-la étenn,
chayé mwen avan syèl-la bwilé"
(take me away before the heavens pass away,
take me away before the skies burn down) — Patrick St. Eloi (1958-2010).

Some rare warbler in the cherries, insistent through the cock-crow,
Sabbath gossip of other birds, distant dogs,
whine of a saw under trees — morning in Plateau, Babonneau;

last night, intimations of death clogged
faith, chills and panic attacked prayer,
every gavel drop of the loud clock

paced the anxious heart peering
away from sleep at corner shadows;
would I lurch against the snorer

swear an incoherent groan
of a farewell, and then, and then...?
            Against indignant protests of the grackles,

gnashing chorus of the barkers, my neighbour turns
up his system on this holy day
shuffling Marley, Patrick

St. Eloi, passed-on chantwelles and their violons, they
I love, gone beyond terrible intimacies of the dark —
            So hear me chantin' loud, see me skank and zouk,

on this green-foliating, bird-bazaaring, Rose-of-Sharon-blooming day.

ix. *The ancient Greeks used four words for love: Storgé, Philia, Eros and Agapé.*

"I have been faithful to thee, Cynara! in my fashion." – Ernest Dowson

    i. Storgé — Family

        Many seem to make a fetish of it
        love of country and family, brandishing flags
        and names with sectarian fervour; but

        not for me, the tedious anthem, the large
        smothering embrace, fragile shells
        which hold tyrannies, cruelties, hard-eyed rages

        against children and thinking citizens – so tell me,
        why that long gaze
        at the relentless torrential avalanche

        of surf; at the golden light on fresh-cut grass
        under mango trees; at the long-time jalousies
        and collapsing fretwork of old Castries;

        at black and white photos of ourselves
        with favourite cousins and dead brothers? –

        Storgé.

    ii. Philia — Friends

        They became few and far-flung
        but once were bosom-close
        before domesticities and schedules

divorced us; nights were laughter-long,
days, pre text and anxious twittering,
waited eager-expectant for those soul-companions

of unspoken covenants we took delight in;
what confidences, what unguarding, what intimacies of trust –
then we scattered to make these sober livings

masked, even in good marriages,
family-responsible, God-fearing –
                that bright-eyed girl, her clean, frank teenage

gaze; those youths under the almonds, passing
whatever they're passing, and giggling;
the cast, after the show, sprawling

over each other on the stage –

Philia.

iii. *Eros – Lovers*

    The flip side: when calls are not taken,
    mounting texts, ignored, obsess you,
    the fewer conversations are reluctant

    and distracted by incessant
    mobile jingles that increase
    your screaming fear across the terrible distance

    lengthening between the recent all-embracing
    sworn recitals of, yes, loving
    it all and this, this casual, care-less

incomprehensible moving
into dimple-deep treachery
and hip-swinging sly slipping

out of reach –
           in the hospital waiting room
an elderly couple are matching

each other, grimace for grimace
as they watch, fingers linked, heads close,
some breaking-news programme –

Eros.

iv. *Agapé – God*

Risky business this – reaching past feelings,
need for attention,
appreciation for work shown as fully

as possible, thanks extended
for gracious gifts made by sacrifice,
and reciprocity expected –

reasonable desires, humanly speaking,
Golden Rule and all that; but the Charity
He commands will surely make

us bitter, gaunt, self-righteous
ghosts of lonely existentialists
in an absurd world – unless

you remember He is thanked less
than anyone else; He is hardly praised
as He deserves; they declared Him dead last

172

century, yet His mercy and His grace
to self-adoring men
are extending greatly still –

Agapé.

x. *(for Pat Ismond 1944-2006)*

"Were your life and work
simply a good translation?" — *Derek Walcott (The Prodigal).*

A translation, Derek, of a kind of odyssey?
Of how I passed and am passing

through this island town
parish of an archipelago nation,

crafting canticles of what I see
metaphors to chant in Kwéyòl melodies

of applauding hordes of surf
cresting the ample bosoms of bays,

of hills smoked blue by early light
and haze of charcoal pits,

of violons, improbable chak-chak benedictions
and chantwelle cantors

with voices like rough-edged, trust-worthy clay;
and the familiar grid of the familiar

city, its streets gossiping memories
of our indiscretions,

small victories, voyages
deaths and divorces

our little books in which they find their lovely names;
not forgetting the journey-man dreams:

republic of arts, theatres and galleries
in pleasant parks and gardens,

the public purse a guarantee
for young painters, dancers, actors,

veterans not neglected
exiled to bitterness and debt —

what do they mean, the life and work
50 years of hours, days and weeks

learning from you and other masters
the magic of line-making

the stitching of stanzas strong
to hold the sly wind of shifting

currents of turning image,
to fish exact nouns with nets flung

at sea-deep roots of our languages,
to handle with care the temperamental conjugations

of verbs that steer our raft and baggage
with stern resolve to some inlet of temporary refuge?

So what is the odyssey,
who is the meaning of this journey —

what signify names of dead lovers
distant friends, dried-up rivers

unknown names of narrow streets
in unfamiliar villages and hamlets

small town fame and passing interest
of the world outside; chapbooks of ambitious verse

forgotten columns and reviews
that stirred forgotten controversies —

this life that presses on
under bird song in the mangoes

crickets in the dark hill, threat of storm, tremblor at 3,
the so-so job, certain faith and safe family

the working of the word
the working of the irrepressible word —

how do they translate?

xi.

"The Sea of Faith
Was once, too at the full, and round earth's shore
Lay like the folds of a bright girdle furled.
But now I only hear
Its melancholy, long, withdrawing roar..."
          – Matthew Arnold ("Dover Beach")

I suppose it's ultimately personal
this building of a life –
ground, wall-block, hardwood, clamped metal roof,
about a well-planted
corner-stone of certain faith –

when the earth-plot shakes to doubt,
window-panes batter in fear against cyclones,
some plump rat rots under the boards
with the stench of horrible news
(you get the point) –

       faith surges like a triumphant vanguard
       of galloping waves off Gros Islet

       to spread its bounteous, cleansing surf
       all along the garbage-littered shore.

xii.
"I dimly guess what Time in mists confounds;
Yet ever and anon a trumpet sounds
From the hid battlements of Eternity;"
    – Francis Thompson (The Hound of Heaven)

When dear, you have gone
far beyond dwarf planets
galaxies of diaphanous nebula
and incomparable deeps
of incredible space –
this one book I have been writing
since you met me in the midday of my journey
confused and without direction
in a maze of deep ravines
and dead rivers,
sucked dry, cast away
by soucouyants and devil women
without remembered names,
and you took me into the house
of your sloe-eyed laughter and your faith
and loved me –
this one book I have been writing
in canticles kwéyòl
dancing lines of lakonmèt and weedova
their violons and chak-chak in my ear,
an epistle of a testament
to your Wonderful King, the Maker of the spheres –
this one book you will see
in His compassionate Hands
and hear Him read for you
the inadequate, untranslatable
unsayable words of my gratitude
for you, my love, my faith companion,
my gift of His incomprehensible grace.

NOTES:

"Line" – pp. 97-101.

The epigraphs are taken from the poetry of the Bible and Derek Walcott.

(ii) "to every line there is a time and a season" comes from "Italian Eclogues", in *The Bounty*.

(iii) "qu'est-ce la poésie... de main en bouche" comes from the French translation of "Forest of Europe", by Claire Malroux, from *The Star-Apple Kingdom* – "what's poetry, if it is worth its salt, but a phrase men can pass from hand to mouth?"

(iv) "but come, girl, get your raincoat... tear-streaked windows" comes from "Piano Practice", in *The Fortunate Traveller*.

(v) "The only art left is the preparation of grace" comes from *The Bounty* – Section Two, #1 (Untitled).

(vi) "I am going down... the same expedition" comes from "Italian Eclogues", in *The Bounty*.

Thanks to Derek Walcott for permission to use these lines from his poems

Other Walcott and St. Lucian references in this poem:

canots – St. Lucian fishing canoes hewn out of gommier trees.

Becune – sea-side location of Derek Walcott's St. Lucian home.

Plateau – in the high hills of Babonneau, north-eastern St. Lucia.

Kabuki – traditional Japanese theatre.

Roddy – Roderick Walcott, twin brother of Derek Walcott, died in 2000.

Brodsky – Russian poet Joseph Brodsky, Nobel prize (1987,) died in 1996.

André Tanker – Trinidadian musician, who composed music for Walcott's plays, died in 2003.

Minshall – Peter Minshall, Trinidadian carnival designer.

Moule à Chique – a rugged and rocky peninsular that forms the southern tip of St. Lucia. It is crested by a lighthouse.

Apilo – nickname of Dunstan St. Omer, St. Lucian painter, lifelong friend of Walcott.

Chantwèl – female lead singer of St. Lucian folk groups.

Soucouyants – vampire-type creature of St. Lucian folklore.

Konserthuset – the Stockholm Concert Hall in which the Nobel Prize ceremony is held.

chak-chak, violon, bones, mandolin – musical instruments used by St. Lucian folk bands.

Kendel Hippolyte, Jane King-Hippolyte, MacDonald Dixon, Fish Alphonse – St. Lucian poets, friends of Walcott.

Choiseul – St. Lucian village, famous for its crafts, like straw baskets (panier).

Majèstwa – St. Lucian Creole word for magistrate, a character in the folk theatre of the flower festivals unique to St. Lucia.

Chantè – male lead singer of St. Lucian folk groups.

Weedova – a St. Lucian folk dance.

Sesenne – St. Lucia's leading folk singer.

"Kwéyòl Canticles", p. 110-111.

Lakonmèt, weedova, scottish etc – traditional folk dances of St. Lucia.

Séwénal – a musical tradition of St. Lucia in which musicians and others with any object that can make a musical sound walk in procession through the town – making music and diverse sounds, of course.

Kwadril (quadrille) – folk dance of St. Lucia, out of the French heritage.

Wob Dwiyèt – national dress of St. Lucian women. The verse describes parts of the dress.

Foulard – a triangular scarf-type part of the wob dwiyèt that is placed over the shoulders. It is usually fastened at the front by a distinctive brooch.

Bandolin – Creole version of mandolin, traditional folk music instrument.

"After Gary Butte", p. 146.

The section titles are from Gary Butte paintings.

ABOUT THE AUTHOR

JOHN ROBERT LEE (b. St. Lucia 1948) has published several collections of poetry. His short stories and poems have been widely anthologised. His reviews and columns have appeared with regularity in newspapers, local and regional. He has also produced and presented radio and television programmes in St. Lucia for many years. His books include *Saint Lucian* (1988), *Artefacts* (2000), *Canticles* (2007), *Elemental* (2008), *Sighting* (2013), *City Remembrances* (2016), *Song and Symphony* (2016). He compiled and edited *Roseau Valley and other poems for Brother George Odlum* (2003), *Bibliography of Saint Lucian Creative Writing 1948-2013* (2013); he co-edited *Saint Lucian Literature and Theatre: an anthology of reviews* (2006) with fellow St. Lucian poet Kendel Hippolyte and co-edited *Sent Lisi: poems and art of Saint Lucia* (2014) with Kendel Hippolyte, Jane King and Vladimir Lucien.

Author Photo by Davina Lee
Cover Art by Gary Butte. 'The Merchant' 2011. Courtesy Nancy Cole-Auguste.

ALSO AVAILABLE BY JOHN ROBERT LEE

elemental
ISBN: 9781845230623; pp. 120; pub. 2008; price £8.99

John Robert Lee brings a quiet, reflective, often autobiographical approach to his concerns with Caribbean life, art and faith.

Within carefully crafted formal structures – and some experimentation with traditional forms – he finds the space to give his voice and persona free rein. Whilst rooted in St. Lucia and Caribbean culture, he takes the whole world as his arena – as much at home writing about Boston as Castries.

Undoubtedly the foremost Caribbean Christian writer of his generation, his is a truly incarnational view of faith, anchored in the reality of human experience and expressed in richly textured images of Caribbean landscapes, dress, street life, music, dance and his native Creole language.